THE LUCIFERIAN
BY
MATHEW EBERTS

"ENLIGHTENED BY THE BLACK FLAME, I WILL FOREVER SERVE MY FATHER LUCIFER. I AM A DEVOTED ADVOCATE OF THE DEVIL, FOR SATAN IS THE ESSENCE OF THE SUN AND HE GAVE ME THE GIFT OF ETERNAL DAMNATION. I AM PERPETUALLY OF SERVICE TO THE FORCES OF DARKNESS, THE DRAGONS OF THE OTHER SIDE."

- MATHEW EBERTS/FRATER LUCIFER

The Testament of Lucifer

I am before all things. I am the God of Gods and there are none like me. I am the Lord of the Power of the Air, the Prince of Darkness and Master of Magicians. I am the Lord of the Earth and the Ruler of the World. I am the Power and the Knowledge. I am the Ancient One, before me was made nothing! I am known by many names. My throne is made of gold, diamonds and stones. I am the Alpha and Omega. I am the Horned God of the Witches and the Black Man of the Sabbat. I am the Ruler of Thaumiel, the Dark Horned Lord of the Qliphoth! I am the Great Red Dragon of the Other Side. I am the Antichrist Spirit and I am the consort of Lilith, the Queen of the Night and the Father of Azazel, he who the Hebrews fear. I am the most powerful God you will ever meet. No man who meets my gaze can withstand the truth of my power. I was, am now and shall have no end. I am ever present to help all who trusts in me and call on me in time of need.
I am Lucifer, the Ruler of Hell.

Table of Contents

1.) Introduction
2.) Lucifer
3.) Luciferian Gnosis
4.) Ritual of Doom
5.) Rituals
6.) Invocations
7.) Conjurations
8.) Incantations to Open the Gates of Hell
9.) Power Meditations
10.) Spells and Sigils to Manifest Desires
11.) The Infernal Spirits
12.) Pacts With the Devil
13.) The Devil's Keys

Chapter 1: Introduction

    Spiritual Luciferianism is the belief that Lucifer is the true Creator God of humanity and the story of the Fallen Angels is true. As the Ruler of Thaumiel, Emperor Lucifer is a Draconian entity, meaning he is one of the Dragons of the Other Side. The Other Side (Sitra Ahra) is the composition of the realms of evil, also known as the Qliphoth, which is where Demons and human spirits reside. There are 11 different realms of the Qliphoth, but Thaumiel is one Realm with two Rulers.

- These are the names of the Eleven Qliphoth, with Daath being a secret realm:

1.) Nahemoth/Lilith — Whisperers, Ruled by Naamah

2.) Gamaliel — The Obscene Ones, Ruled by Lilith

3.) Samael — Poison of God, Ruled by Adramelech

4.) A'arab Zaraq — Ravens of Dispersion, Ruled by Ba'al

5.) Thagirion — The Disputers, Ruled by Belphegor

6.) Golachab — Burning Bodies, Ruled by Asmodeus/Samael

7.) Gha'ag-Sheblah — The Smiters, Ruled by Astarot

8.) Daath — The Abyss (Secret Realm), Ruled by Choronzon

9.) Satariel — The Concealers, Ruled by Lucifuge Rofocale

10.) Ghagiel — The Hinderers, Ruled by Belzebud

11.) Thaumiel — The Twin Gods, Ruled by Satan and Molok

The Qliphoth is identified with the Tree of Knowledge from the Garden of Eden. It is the opposite and shadow side of the Sephiroth, the Tree of Life, which are realms of angels. The Tree of Death is indeed the one you want when you want demonic power and knowledge. The Dark Tree is ruled by Demons, the Original Pagan Gods. Satan Lucifer and his Demons are wonderful when treated with respect. Most of the content in Christian grimoires, such as Grimoirium Verum and the Grand Grimoire, are disrespectful towards these entities because they use ancient Hebrew names of the enemy god, so I advise you not to use them.

I find the conjurations within this book to be neutral respect-wise. I use my own conjurations which are edited from the grimoires, but I find them to work better because I used some different words of power for them and used good English asking help from these Demons.

The Qliphoth's beliefs are nowhere closely associated with Judaism. It's Left Hand Path Occult Practices except it uses Hebrew, Sumerian and Latin incantations, phrases and words of power. The techniques may be Hebrew, but Hebrew is a magical language in itself. Satan, Astarot, Samael/Ashmedai, Azazel, Lilith, Naamah, Molok, Belial, Ba'al and Leviatan are all Hebrew names for Demons. That's why the Qliphoth's language is Hebrew, is because the Qliphoth's Demons' names are in Hebrew. Hebrew is a very ancient and magical language. There are many words of power, incantations, invocations and conjurations in Hebrew within the Qliphoth's Magic. All of the Qliphothic Grimoires I've used mainly used were Hebrew conjurations since the Qliphothic Realms are also Hebrew! I'm glad I was originally Jewish before becoming a Satanist/Luciferian/Draconian Sorcerer because I already know Hebrew and it assists me in speaking it correctly when I use Qliphothic Grimoires.

Here is a diagram of the of the Qliphoth:

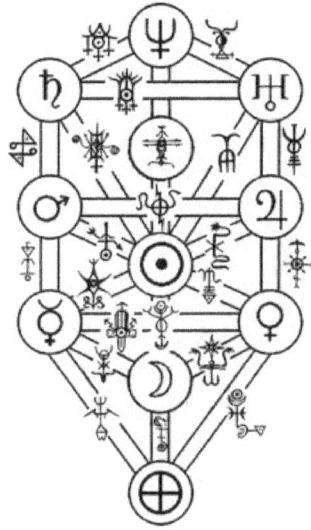

You have to work your way from the bottom of the Qliphothic Tree to the top. Once you reach Thaumiel, you are given the Promise of the Serpent, which is ascension to godhood. Lucifer, also called Satan, the Ruler of Thaumiel, was the Serpent in the Garden of Eden. Luciferianism is basically a mature form of Satanism that embraces enlightenment and self-deification; the quest for knowledge and power. Working with the Qliphoth is a hard thing to do, because Demons can test your faith, knowledge and devotion.

"This calls for wisdom, let the one who has understanding calculate the number of the beast, for it is the number of a man, and his number is 666."

The number 666 is not only the number of the

Antichrist, but it is also the Kabbalistic square root of the Sun. Lucifer is the pre-Christian Pagan Sun God, which makes sense regarding how 666 is one of his numbers.

666 is everlasting life and spiritual/physical perfection.

Chapter 2: Lucifer

Lucifer, the Morning Star, the Prince of Darkness, is the Spirit of Enlightenment and Liberation. His day is Monday, but his most personal day of the year is December 23, which is to be observed by every dedicated Luciferian and Satanist. Satan's colors are blue, black and red. Lucifer has a fiery red appearance most of the time. He may wear a red cloak or red armor. Lucifer's numbers are 2, 4, 11, 13 and 666. His directions are both East and South, which is where your altar should be facing. I prefer setting up my Satanic Luciferian Altar in the East, since that is where the Sun rises. Lucifer's planets are the Sun, Uranus, and Venus. His Zodiac Signs are Leo, Capricorn, and Aquarius. Animals that are sacred to Satan are the Dragon, the Lion, the Goat, the Raven, the Peacock and the Serpent. Lucifer is the Necronomicon God Ea/Enki, but also Nyarlathotep, the Black Man of the Sabbat, Messenger of the Gods. Enki means, "Lord of the

Earth" and he is also known as Melek Ta'us, Baphomet, Prometheus, Iblis, Asturel, Pan, Helel Ben Shachar and Ra-Hoor-Khuit. Lucifer has various different names from different cultures. I think I even missed a few, but I named what I could. There is a short phrase to use in rituals that is a short calling to Lucifer. It's called a Demonic Enn, which are short phrases of invocation to a particular spirit.

Lucifer's Demonic Enn is "Renich tasa uberaca biasa icar Lucifer."

Sigil of Luciferian Witchcraft

Lucifer has many forms and appears in many different ways. On the Left Hand Path, we encounter him as the Infernal Emperor of Sitra Ahra. Lucifer's sin was pride, which was why he was cast down to Hell. In medieval grimoires, Lucifer is the the Emperor of Hell, the Emperor ruling the entire infernal hierarchy. He rules the elements fire and air. Lucifer's energy is electrifying and very powerful. It's like being shocked in a comfortable way. Lucifer does not hate humanity, he hates the Judeo-Christian God Jehova and the Nazarene Yeshua. He actually rebelled against God because he wanted to help humanity become as Gods. Lucifer is a shape-shifter, which means he can appear in any form. I think it has a lot to do with how your mind wants to process his appearance.

Lucifer is very real and this is how Lucifer appears to me:

Lucifer has shown me Hell and it's not a bad place at all. In fact, he can make a Heaven out of Hell for you. You will be a Demon yourself, if you follow instructions on my methods of self-deification. Satan already blesses us with a Demonic Soul from birth,

AND FOR THOSE THAT ARE DESCENDANTS OF SATAN ALREADY HAVE THESE POWERS, BUT NEED HELP LEARNING HOW TO USE THEM. MY METHODS ARE VERY EASY, YOU JUST GOT TO DO IT AND BEFORE YOU KNOW IT, YOU'LL HAVE GODLIKE POWERS. I COMBINE METHODS FROM NOTORIOUS LEFT HAND PATH OCCULT PRACTITIONERS. THESE TECHNIQUES I USE ARE VERY POTENT. CERTAIN TECHNIQUES I USE DAILY ARE WORDS OF POWER IN INVOCATIONS AND RITUALS, YOGA, MAGIC TRANCES, MEDITATIONS AND DIVINATION.

THIS IS LUCIFER'S CALLING FORMULA:

MED-ORTH + LUCIFERO + LUMIEL + HELEL BEN SHACHAR + LUCIBEL + ASTUREL + AGGELOS PHOS + LIFTOACH KLIFFOT + LIFTOACH PANDEMONIUM

My invocations, conjurations, rituals and meditations are potent, so you should be a dedicated Luciferian or Satanist before attempting these things. A dedicated Luciferian has successfully signed a blood pact with Lucifer. Methods on pact-making with Lucifer are discussed in Chapter 12. When you are on the correct path, the Left Hand Path, you are revealed to things that are unknown to the masses. Satan and his Demons give you hidden secrets and powers you never knew you had in you, such as telekinesis, pyrokinesis, electrokinesis and telepathy. You become a living God, with true powers of the mind/soul with true Satanic or Luciferian Gnosis and Powers. Along with the abilities stated above, you are also conjuring spirits that will help you further advance on the Path of the Wise. This book will assist you with many things that are associated with the Left Hand Path.

Chapter 3: Luciferian Gnosis

Luciferian Gnosis is knowledge and wisdom of everything that has to do with Lucifer. I do believe the more you know has a lot to do with how much you are interested in a particular thing. For example, Lucifer is everything you want him to be. He can do marvelous things for you. You just have to let him into your heart, mind, body and soul. It's through a pact with Lucifer you will learn from Lucifer himself. He makes the best teacher and guide. He bestows Luciferian Gnosis upon you as long as you take his hand and let him guide you through Hell. Lucifer inspires those who want to do his Will on Earth. In this Chapter, I will get to discussing what ritual tools are and the purpose behind them, magic symbols used by Luciferians, certain prayers to Lucifer, Demonic Magic Conjurations and the overall knowledge of spiritual mysteries.

•

Symbols

The Inverted Pentagram is used by Satanists and Luciferians to represents evil, dark sinister magic, and the Left Hand Path. It is the Horned Head of Lucifer, It is a key to the currents of the Nightside. It also represents the five elements (Earth, Air, Fire, Water and Spirit).

The 11-pointed Star represents the Qliphoth. It can be used as a gateway to the currents of the Qliphoth. The eleven points represents the eleven different realms of the Qliphoth.
(Artwork Courtesy: Asenath Mason)

THE EYE OF LUCIFER IS A POPULAR OCCULT SYMBOL. THE EYE REPRESENTS THE CENTER OF AWAKENED CONSCIOUSNESS AND CORRESPONDS TO THE THIRD EYE. THE TRIANGLE REPRESENTS THE FIRE ELEMENT.

 THE SIGIL OF LUCIFER IS THE MOST IMPORTANT OCCULT SYMBOL USED IN LUCIFERIANISM. YOU SHOULD HAVE AN IMAGE OF THIS SIGIL SOMEWHERE ON YOUR ALTAR.

THE SERPENT IS SYMBOLIC OF

LUCIFER IN THE GARDEN OF EDEN. LUCIFER TEMPTED EVE TO EAT THE FRUIT FROM THE TREE OF KNOWLEDGE OF GOOD AND EVIL.

THE GREAT RED DRAGON IS A TITLE FOR LUCIFER. THE SEVEN-HEADED DRAGON IS SYMBOLIC OF LEVIATAN OR TIAMAT.

BAPHOMET IS SYMBOLIC OF LUCIFER AND IT'S VERY IMPORTANT TO HAVE A BAPHOMET STATUE OR SIGIL OF BAPHOMET SOMEWHERE ON YOUR ALTAR.

Ritual Tools

Altar and ritual tool consecration must take place on a full moon.

Altar - The altar is what you keep all your ritual tools and symbols on. It's where you stand to do rituals involving invocations and evocations.

Write this prayer on the back of a piece of paper with a printed Sigil of Lucifer on it:

"Lord Lucifer, in your name, I implore you to be favorable and bless this sacred space. I ask you send your Demons to guard this sacred space. I ask you to come here yourself and bestow upon me the power to make this my personal Temple of the Devil on the Path of Self-Deification. Ave Lucifer!"

After you write the prayer, conduct a Standard Ritual to Lucifer, reading out the prayer and burning it in the flame of a red candle. After you burn the prayer, you can meditate for fifteen minutes while chanting this phrase of words of power:

"ZON GATH AM SADAM – ZAMRAN!"

Athame - The ritual blade is used to command and invoke spirits. The Athame is traditionally black-handled, to represent the Forces of Darkness. To consecrate the Athame, say this while holding the ritual blade over the incense:

"In the name of Lucifer, I consecrate and initiate this Element of Air! May the Forces of Darkness enter in through the blade and into my soul to empower it! May every aspect of my self strengthen and powers magnify by tenfold!"

Wand - A Wand, like the Athame, is used to command and invoke spirits. My Wand is made of Oak, because Oak wood is all-purpose for spirits.

Recite this phrase to consecrate the Wand while holding the Wand with both hands over the incense:

"By the name of the Scarlet Whore, by the name of the Jew who will always ignore, by the dreadful sounds of an unholy prayer, in the name of Lucifer, the Lord of the Air, I consecrate this Wand and may the power of The Seven enter into it."

Bell - A bell is rang before and after each ritual to signify the beginning and the end.

Chalice - The liquid in the chalice is drank after each invocation to take in the spirit.

To consecrate the Chalice, recite this phrase while holding the Chalice over incense smoke:

"In the name of Lucifer, I bless and dedicate this instrument of Water. With each drink, I take in the spirit of all the demonic power I need to thrive on."

Candles - Candles and their colors are used in magic. Typically for Luciferianism, the candle colors should be either blue, black or red: the colors of Lucifer. I prefer using one red and one black candle in my rituals, since Lucifer appeared to me as a black man in a red robe.

SCRYING MIRROR - A black magic mirror is good for seeing and communicating with spirits. Scrying mirrors are a divination tool for looking into past lives, but also past, present and future events. The black scrying mirror, also known as the "magic mirror" is a powerful metaphysical tool.

BAPHOMET STATUE - The Baphomet Statue is symbolic of Lucifer.

SIGILS - Every Altar should at least have the Sigil of Lucifer on it. If you want to have more sigils than just the Sigil of Lucifer, then go for it.

After you get done consecrating all your ritual tools, recite the Third Devil's Key.

ABOVE: MY SATANIC-LUCIFERIAN ALTAR WHICH HAS VARIOUS SIGILS, RITUAL TOOLS AND BOOKS OF MAGIC ON IT.

Prayers

Dawn Prayer
Hail unto thee who art thou Spiritual Sun in thy rising, Satan, the only one who can fulfill my desires! You, who stirs the senses, break the shells to the Realms of the Nightside. At the beginning of this day, Lord Satan, I ask that you protect me and assist me in my endeavors. This, I humbly ask in your name Father Lucifer. By the words I speak, so let it be thus! EXAT, KAKAMA AMANU!

Noon Prayer
Oh thou Beautiful Spirit of Rebellion, Initiator of the Way, Angel and Devil, Saint and Beast, Lucifer, Morning Star of the East! In this Noontide Hour, I pray thee the power to execute my endeavors. Give me the knowledge and strength to rule over my own reality. Make me that witch who shines bright like the Sun today. By the words I speak, so let it be thus! EXAT, KAKAMA AMANU!

Dusk Prayer
As the Sun goes down and the Stars shine in the Darkness, I ask you, Lucifer, the Bringer of the Light, the Lord of the Night to give me the gift of the Evening Twilight. Thank you, Lucifer, for the gifts you have bestowed upon me today, for teaching me ancient ways and for the pleasures in which I have partaken. EXAT, KAKAMA AMANU!

Midnight Prayer
Hail unto Thee who art thou Spiritual Sun in thy hiding! Lucifer, Prince of Darkness, Infernal Emperor, guide me to your palace in the Void! Break the shells of Sitra Ahra so that I may enter the

Nightside Realms! Satan, Ruler of Thaumiel, may I forever be within the Realms of Evil? May I be forever within these contending forces? By the words I speak, so let it be thus! By the words I speak, so let it be thus! EXAT, KAKAMA AMANU!

Demonic Magic Conjurations

These are short phrases to be uttered in a chant during meditation or with a wave of a Wand either during ritual or in front of someone or something you desire.

To bring money: Onaim, Perantes, Rasonatos.

Seduction: Nades, Suradis, Maniner.

Better health: Reterrem, Salibat, Crateres, Hisater.

Win contests: Rokes, Pulatus, Zotoas, Tulitas, Xatanitos.

Bring women: Sadar, Prostas, Solaster.

Against curses: Senapos, Terfita, Estamos, Notarin.

Invisibility: Benatir, Cararaku, Dedos, Etinarmi.

Revenge: Osthariman, Visantiparos, Noctatur.

Any desire: Zorami, Zaitux, Elastot.

See into another's mind: O Tarot, Nizael, Estarnos, Tantarez.

Reward friends: Nista, Saper, Visnos.

World travel: Raditus, Polastrien, Terpandu, Ostrata, Pericatur, Ermas.

Learn secrets: Nitrae, Radou, Sunandam.

Demonic Power: Actatos, Catipta, Bejouran, Itapan, Marnutus.

Gnosis

The Four Great Rulers of Sitra Ahra to be invoked during ritual:

East - Lucifer
North - Lilith
West - Tiamat aka Leviatan
South - Asmodeus aka Samael

The Four Crowned Princes of Hell to be invoked during ritual:

East - Satan
North - Belzebud
West - Astarot
South - Azazel

You can either invoke the Four Great Rulers or the Four Crowned Princes during each ritual. When I'm working with the Qliphoth, I invoke the Four Great Rulers of the Sitra Ahra, but when I'm just doing a Standard Satanic Luciferian Ritual, I invoke the Four Crowned Princes of Hell. There is a big difference, so let's say you're using Asenath Mason's grimoires for working with the Qliphoth, such as Tree of Qliphoth or Qliphothic Meditations, you would first invoke the Four Great Rulers of Sitra Ahra. Even the Simon Necronomicon is a Qliphothic grimoire, so before using the Necronomicon, invoke Lucifer, Lilith, Leviatan and Samael and they will assist you in raising your Kundalini Force.

These are the gates to higher levels of consciousness and words of passage to obtain these higher levels of consciousness:

The first gate is pain. The word of passage is ZIRLAT. The offering is blood. The reward is communication with Demons.

The second gate is fear. The word of passage is RAMADAN. The offering is urine. The reward is a good demonic personality.

The third gate is despair. The word of passage is ZIRAM. The offering is saliva. The reward is knowledge.

The fourth gate is madness. The word of passage is ADENATA. The offering is sweat. The reward is precognition and other psychic abilities.

The fifth gate is fury. The word of passage is GALAD. The offering are semen and vaginal fluid. The reward is gnosis and power.

Sex Magic

Sex Magic is the art of creating magic or obtaining magical results through sexual intercourse.

"Sodomy is especially sacred to Set because It opens what are called the Typhonion tunnels, channels through which extremely powerful demons, like the horrible Choronzon, can travel from the alternate reality and emerge into this universe and enter the sex partner's body."
-Wicca, Satan's Little White Lie. pages 192, 197-200

Ritual sodomy stimulates what is called the Kundalini gland, which acts to stimulate the pineal gland. Some use drugs like peyote, mescaline or DMT for a similar experience, but ritual sodomy is the preferred means that appears to have no real substitute. There is a powerful ritual sex magick that was practiced by the ancients and is practiced today, which still manifests a powerful transformative supernaturalism! The act of sodomy is also performed to open up the initiate's third eye which is suppose to enhance psychic ability. During this act, a Demonic entity called Legion, is invoked, referred to as an unclean spirit. The key is in the trauma: the complete destruction of the inner spirit. Then at the propitious moment the initiate's third eye is opened so as to completely re-socialize them and open their psychic abilities. In doing so, a bridge is created between this physical world and the spiritual realm. Once the Pineal

Gland is opened, it allows a person to see into that realm. Thus, the reference to it being the Third Eye. To fully open the third eye to see into the spiritual realm, you must do the Opening the Third Eye exercises in Chapter 10.

"Those Sons of Mighty Satan who practice the dark occult arts believe and preach proudly to the world that Sodomy is a vehicle through which the door is open to the spiritual realm."

Sodomy is not a requirement in opening your third eye and communicating with Fallen Angels. Though, what is a requirement is doing the meditations that are outlined in this book in order to open and empower the chakras.

The Ritual of Doom is a remake of The Bornless Ritual written by Mathew Eberts/Frater Lucifer, which is a ritual employed in order to make contact with your Guardian Demon and to grow closer to Lucifer the Satan.

Chapter 4: The Ritual of Doom

Thee I invoke, The Evil One,

Thee that didst create the Earth and the Seven Heavens, Thee that didst create the Night and the Day, Thee that didst create the Darkness and the Light, Thou art Satan, whom only your Prophets hath seen! Thou art the mighty Morning Star! Thou art the Serpent of Paradise! Thou hast distinguished between the Just and the Unjust! Thou didst make the Female and the Male! Thou didst produce the Seeds and the Fruit! Thou didst form men to love one another, and to hate one another! I am (NAME OF MAGICIAN), Thy Prophet, unto whom thou didst commit thy mysteries, the Ceremonies of Hell. Thou didst produce the good and the bad, and that which nourisheth all of your Creation! Hear thou me, for I am the son/daughter of Lucifer! This is thy true name, handed down to the Prophets of Sitra Ahra. Hear me: AR; NODON; THULE; VRIL; ADASET; NIAK; AZOA; ZOVAS; ZOVAN; UL; THIAN. Hear me, and make all Spirits subject unto Me, so that every Spirit of the Firmament and of the Ether, upon the Earth and under the Earth, on dry Land and in the Water, of whirling Air, or of rushing Fire, and every Spell and Scourge of God may be obedient unto Me! I invoke Thee, the Shining One, who dwellest in the Void Place of the Spirit: AMELETH; SATAN; ABRAZKA; FALARTHIAN; KUNDA; NARDAR; The Evil One: Hear me! Hear me: RUAZO; THIAO; ZO-AN-SHU-SET; ADONAI; AFENIAK; SA; EDA; LOHOLO; ABRAXAS; ASADAM; ROBRIAM! Mighty and Powerful One! Hear me! I invoke Thee: NYARLATHOTEP; ORION; CAELAZOD; KAMERON; AGERATH; ALOGOS; Hear me! Hear me! ABRAZKA; CANAN; SABAI; INFERNUM! This is the Lord of the Gods: This is the Lord of the Universe: This is He whom the Winds fear: This is He who having made Voice by his Commandment is Lord of all Things: King, Ruler, and Helper, Hear me! Hear me: OUIA; DUMOSON; VONTON; MAHAZEL; ALEGREMOS; NADA; ABADON; AKSAFAT; AZA; ZODAMETA; ATUSIR; EDE; EDU; DAIMON TON THEON; LAM; SODIERNO; DUMASO; NOARD; TELOCVOVIM VOVIN! I am He! The Antichrist Spirit, having sight in the Feet, Strong, and the Immortal Fire! I am He, the Truth! I am He, who hates the angels which should be wrought in the World! I am He, that lightningeth and thundereth! I am He, from whom is the Shower of the Life of Earth! I am He, whose mouth ever flameth! I am He, the Begetter and Manifester unto the Light! I am He, the Grace of the World! "THE WITCH WITH A POWERFUL SOUL" is my name! Come thou forth, and follow me, and make all Spirits subject unto Me, so that every Spirit of the Firmament and of the Ether, upon the Earth and under the Earth, on dry Land or in the Water, of whirling Air or of rushing Fire, and every Spell and Scourge of God will be obedient to Me!

NUTAR; SORONOS! Such are the words!

Ya Namosh Panachasragoth Exat!

THE EFFECTS OF THE RITUAL OF DOOM:

- COMMUNION WITH LUCIFER
- SUBMISSIVENESS OF FALLEN ANGELS
- POSSIBLE ASTRAL SEX WITH FALLEN ANGELS
- POWERS AND GNOSIS FROM FALLEN ANGELS

CHAPTER 5: RITUALS

FOR EVERY DRACONIAN RITUAL, YOU MUST BE DRESSED IN ALL BLACK AND YOUR ALTAR MUST BE FACING EAST.

STANDARD DRACONIAN LUCIFERIAN RITUAL

RING THE BELL, TURNING COUNTER-CLOCKWISE, INVOKE THE FOUR CROWNED PRINCES OF HELL USING THE ATHAME OR OAK WAND IN YOUR LEFT HAND.

EAST - SATAN
NORTH - BELZEBUD
WEST - ASTAROT
SOUTH - AZAZEL

Recite the Invocation to Lucifer:

In nomine Draco, quo veniat satanas Lucifer!

In the name of Lucifer, Ruler of the Earth, Fallen Angel and our lord Devil, who has created man to reflect in Thine own image and likeness, I invite the Forces of Sitra Ahra to bestow their infernal power upon me! Open the Gates of the Qliphoth to come forth to greet me as your friend. Deliver me, Lord Satan, from all past error and delusion. Fill me with power and truth. Keep me strong in my faith and service to the Infernal Empire, that I may abide in praise. Glory and joy everylasting forevermore!

- Drink from Chalice

- Read the written prayer to Father Lucifer and burn it in the flame of a blue, black or red candle, then place it in the silver burning bowl.

- Power meditate for at least 15 minutes

- After meditation, communicate with Lucifer telepathically.

- Recite proper Enochian Key

- Say "Ave Lucifer!"

- Turn clockwise and ring the Bell.

                    END

Thanksgiving Ritual

This ritual is the same as the Standard Luciferian Ritual, except you write out a prayer thanking Lucifer for what he has done for you.

Destruction Ritual

Ring the Bell, turning counter-clockwise, invoke the Four Crowned Princes of Hell using the Destruction Athame in your left hand.

East - Satan
North - Belzebud
West - Astarot
South - Azazel

RECITE THE INVOCATION TO LUCIFER:

IN NOMINE DRACO, QUO VENIAT SATANAS LUCIFER!

IN THE NAME OF LUCIFER, RULER OF THE EARTH, DEVIL AND ANGEL, WHO HAS CREATED MAN TO REFLECT IN THINE OWN IMAGE AND LIKENESS, I INVITE THE FORCES OF SITRA AHRA TO BESTOW THEIR INFERNAL POWER UPON ME! OPEN THE GATES OF THE SITRA AHRA TO COME FORTH TO GREET ME AS YOUR FRIEND. YOU DWELL IN THE HEART OF MAN, DESIRING TO DELIVER KNOWLEDGE AND TRUTH TO YOUR FAITHFUL. DELIVER ME, LORD LUCIFER, FROM ALL PAST ERROR AND DELUSION. FILL ME WITH GNOSIS, POWER AND TRUTH. KEEP ME STRONG IN MY FAITH AND SERVICE TO THE INFERNAL EMPIRE, THAT I MAY ABIDE WITH PRAISE. GLORY AND JOY EVERLASTING FOREVERMORE!

- DRINK FROM CHALICE

- READ OUT LOUD THE HANDWRITTEN DESTRUCTION PRAYER OF CHOSEN ENEMY WITH HIS/HER FULL NAME INCLUDED.

- PIERCE THROUGH PRAYER WITH THE ATHAME, THEN BURN THE PRAYER IN THE FLAME OF A CANDLE.

- MEDITATE WHILE USING VISUALIZATION TO TORMENT AND HARM HIM/HER.

- THANK THE FORCES OF DARKNESS FOR THEIR HELP.

- Recite the Tenth Enochian Key

- Turn clockwise and ring the Bell.

- Take the burned remains and flush them down the toilet.

- Clean your aura

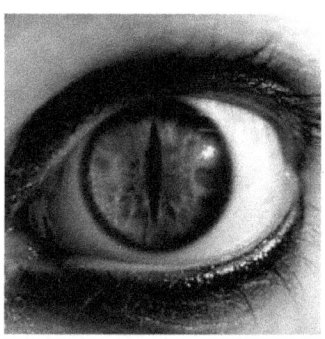

Death Spell

This is only for an enemy you wish would just die. Make sure the person you are putting the spell on is the person you want to do this to, because there is no reversing this spell. Once they die, they're dead forever or will be incapacitated for the rest of their life.

*Personal belongings should be used.

- Construct an effigy or a poppet using the personal belongings

- Go to a cemetery and get some dirt.

- Vent into the poppet, visualizing the victim, using all the hate possible, especially during its construction. It is imperative to stay focused with intent. This is best done during a waning moon, most preferably when the moon is in Scorpio or Capricorn.

- Construct a small box or coffin to put the poppet in.

- Light a black candle.

- Concentrate intensely upon the death and destruction of the enemy. DO NOT BE DISTURBED OR LOSE FOCUS!

- Put the effigy into its box

- Bury it in the graveyard dirt inside the box, but save some of the cemetery dirt.

- Take it outside, or back to the graveyard and bury it, placing the reserved dirt on top of the box knowing the victim will meet his/her death.

-DO NOT think about the spell or the enemy, as this will interfere with the working.

- Clean your aura and your chakras.

- FORGET IT EVER HAPPENED

END

Summoning the Four Demonic Rulers of Sitra Ahra

(Face the Altar, chanting ZAZAS ZAZAS NASATANADA ZAZAS until you feel ready to proceed with the ritual)

Liftoach shaari Ha-Thaumiel B-Shem ha-Satan va-Molok!(x11)

In the name of the Devil, Prince and Master of the Rebellious Spirits, I summon you: the Dark Rulers of Sitra Ahra! Hear my voice beckon and come forth!

SOUTH: I invoke you, Asmodeus! Lord of the Southern Watchtower! Come to me, Poison of God! Light up the darkness with your fire and let me become enlightened!

EAST: I invoke you, Lucifer! Lord of the Eastern Watchtower! Come to me mighty Morning Star! Reveal to me the ancient wisdom that you have guarded since the beginning!

NORTH: I invoke you, Lilith! Goddess of the Northern Watchtower! Come to me Dark Witch of Gamaliel! Whisper to me the forgotten secrets of darkness in which I dedicate myself!

WEST: I invoke you, Tiamat! Goddess of the Western Waters! Come to me, Dragon from the Sea! Mother of Lucifer, lead me to your waters, out of which the whole universe emerged!

FACING THE ALTAR: Come thou forth Ancient Ones! I summon you from your dwelling place, from the spaces between light and darkness! Come to me through the Tunnels of Set!

  SARAF ADONAI SAMAEL!
  LUCIFER, LIFTOACH PANDEMONIUM!
  RENICH VIASA AVAGE LILITH LIRACH!
  HEI ELU TIAMAT!

ZAZAS ZAZAS NASATANADA ZAZAS! ZROSA NANNAT HEKA RASA!
LEPACA KLIFFOT, MARAG TEHOM NOGAR KAMUSIL LEVIATAN NAGID THELI!
JADEN TASA HOET NACA LEVIATAN!

THADEKIEL + ABRAXIEL + MAHAZIEL + AZAZAeL + LUFUGIEL! HAIL SATAN!

THE MIDNIGHT GAME

The midnight Game is a test of faith and devotion to the Left Hand Path. It is a game, a spell, an invocation, a nightmare... It should only be done by those who are experienced. There is a high risk of mental scarring and can even result in death, so be very careful!

Players:
- At least 1 player minimal

Requirements per person:
- 1 candle
- 1 lighter or book of matches
- 1 piece of paper
- 1 writing implement
- 1 pin
- 1 wooden door, closed
- Salt

Instructions:

The Invitation:

1. Begin prior to midnight.

2. Write your full name — first, middle, and last — on the piece of paper with your writing implement. Prick your finger with the pin and squeeze until a drop of blood appears. Dot the blood on the paper and allow it to soak in.
3. Turn off every light in your home.
4. Place the paper with your name and blood on it in front of the closed wooden door. Light the candle using the matches or lighter and place it on top of the paper. If you are using a taper, make sure it is placed in a candle holder .

5. Knock on the door 22 times. The final knock must occur precisely when the clock chimes 12am. Open the door; then blow out the candle and close the door.
6. Relight your candle immediately.

The Main Event:
1. Keeping your candle in hand and your salt and matches or lighter close by, begin to move about your home.
2. Should your candle go out, you must relight it within the next ten seconds. If you are successful, continuing moving about your home. Do not stop moving until 3:33am.
3. If you are unsuccessful in relighting the candle, immediately surround yourself with a circle of salt. Remain inside the circle until 3:33am.

The Ending:
1. At 3:33am, it is safe to stop moving or to step outside your circle of salt. You may also turn on the lights. The game is over.

If you survived through the game, you know you won. Congratulations, you beat The Midnight Game.

Ritual of Lucifer and Lilith

Lucifer, Nyarlathotep, Samyaza, Iblis, SATAN! Lilit, Ardat-Lili, Laylah, Layil, LILITH! Liftoach Pandemonium! Liftoach Kliffot!

In the name of the Dragon, I call upon Lucifer and Lilith for the purpose of unholy communion! YID CHES MUN NAG LAM SAT AN! Lucifer, grant me the power to rule the world! Lilith, grant me the power to create!

ATHAH GIBOR LAY-OLAM SATAN! LUCIFER ILLUMINATIO MEA!

Satan and Lilith, Parents of all Demons, may you find my soul, mind and body as your own Demonic child! Lilith, Lady of Blood and Witchcraft, let my grace fall! Lucifer, damn me to Hell, Father of the Demonic All! May the fire of the Infernal Dragon flow through my veins! Lucifer! Lilith! Devil-Man! Demon-Woman! Let my will be fulfilled through your dark gifts! Transform my consciousness and light the black flame of dark illumination in my soul!

I call to you both in the name of the Dragon!

Hail Lucifer! Hail Lilith!

Ritual of the Black Flame

ZAZAS ZAZAS NASATANADA ZAZAS! Open, open, gates of Hell, open!

LIFTOACH KLIFFOT! ATAZOT! ZO AN SHU SAMYAZA!
I am the Master of the Demons, the unconquered Ruler of the World! Lucifer, embrace my soul and allow me to submit myself to you! Your Black Flame burns brightly, engulfing my weakness and transforming my soul! I am a child of the Great Red Dragon of the Other Side!

Bagabi Laca Bachabe Lamac Lamec Bachalyas Cabahagy Sabalyos Baryolos Lagoz Atha Cabyolas Samahac Et Famyolas Harrahya!

I invoke and harness all demonic energy and forces to use at my will! May my Father Lucifer give me the Black Flame which I can use to my best advantage!

ACTEUS MAGELSIUS ORMENUS LYCAS NICON MIMON!

I AM THE TEMPLE OF ALL GODS, THE OMNIPRESENT STARRY ONE, THE ONE SPIRIT, FOUNT OF ALL SORCERY! ALO VET ZIRAM, I CALL THE SECRET OF THE CONJUNCTION OF THE SUN AND THE MOON

APIERIATUR TERRA ET GERMINET LUCIFER!
 KARU SAMSU!

  EE SCARA VARCHE, NARTAR!

    AZOTOZ!

Chapter 6: Invocations

The following are invocations of powerful fallen angels known as "The Seven". The Seven include Satan Lucifer, Belial, Leviatan/Tiamat, Azazel, Asmodeus/Samael, Astarot, and Belzebud. There are also more invocations towards the next chapter of evocations or conjurations.

Invocation of Lucifer

NAMATADA ABEKO ORIET!

Renich tasa uberaca biasa icar Lucifer! (x11)

I call upon Lucifer to guide me as I walk the backwards path of the Devil! I call you, Lucifer, the Light Bringer, Devil of Blood Oaths and legends of temptations. Prince of Darkness and Infernal Emperor, come to me! Lord of the Air, I open the gates of the East as I seek power, not to be scared! Before the almighty and ineffable Lucifer the Infernal Emperor, who I invite into my flesh, I hail the Lord of Thaumiel! Transform me through your dark and forbidden alchemy! Guide me on the Serpent Path to the heart of your Throne! Make me into Thy powerful servant and perform your magical alchemy on my soul! Answer to the words of power!

Med-Orth + Lucifero + Lumiel + Helel ben Shachar + Lucibel + Asturel + Aggelos Phos + Liftoach Qliphoth + Liftoach Pandemonium!

Emperor Lucifer, whom I call the mighty Lord Satan, Prince and Master of the rebellious spirits, condescend to be favorable — so it shall be!
Ruler of Thaumiel, the almighty god Satan, I implore you to abandon your dwelling to come speak with me!

Thaninel + Akzarel + Uazarel + Mibdalahel + Ianahel + Abadel + Labahel + [Liftoach shaari ha-Thaumiel B'Shem ha-Satan va-Molok! (x11)]

Akal Esh—Shachar + Theli + Elyon + Samael Acher + Nachash Hakadmoni + Melech ha-Melachim ha-Aur She-Ain Bo Machshavah + Gibor Helel Satan + Liftoach Kliffot!

Come Lucifer, come! I invite you to come forth!

Ol um isli das ol zodameta, Lucifer, micalzo uransee gah o a Ror, Zil odzamran caosg!

Ol bolape de Lucifer casarma sonuf paid!

Ol bolape a el casarma bolape olapireta!

Ol zir a noco de Satan!

Zarrafrom!

Invocation of Belial

Lirach tasa vefa wehl Belial!

King Belial, the wicked one, answer me and heed the call! Leader of the Sons of Darkness! Angel of Enmity! Your counsel is to bring about wickedness and guilt! Ruler of this World! Matanbuchus, the one without a master! I invoke Thee, Belial! Meet me at the Gate and reveal to me the secrets of the Unseen! Guide me on the path of darkness unto light, through the Place of Crossing, at the threshold of the Nightside! Grace me with your guidance and empower my ascent! Belial, he who bows to no man nor to any God. Belial, he who has all power over all dominions, come! King of Demons, lend me your visage, lend me your wisdom and lend me your strength! Come from the realm of Daath and rise up from the depths to grant me power over the living and the dead! Belial, Matanbuchus, I do invoke Thee! I offer my body as a temple for your immortal essence! Let me be your apprentice in magic! Make me into a powerful sorcerer! Make me King of the World as the Devil's child! Master of the Pit, bring forth your wisdom, bring forth your power and bring forth your freedom from the realm of Daath!

Belial Badad, Lepaca Kliffoth, Belial Badad, Lepaca Sitra Ahra!

En dooain i Babalonu!

Invocation of Leviatan/Tiamat

Jedan tasa hoet naca Leviatan! Leviatan, Dragon of the Sea, I conjure thee forth, come to me! Monster of the Apocalypse, reveal to me forgotten knowledge slumbering in my soul! May the Seven-Headed Dragon of the Void guide me on my way to godhood!

VOVIN(x6)

TOHU TEHOM THELI THAN LEVIATAN TANIN'IVER TANINSAM!

I call upon the Dragon of the Black Earth, Leviatan, the Great Dragon who holds the soul of the world! I invoke your essence into my flesh! Inflame my soul and transform me into a great Dragon myself!

TANIN'IVER LIFTOACH NIA! DESSURPUR KAJP GIDUPP LEVIATAN!

I pray thee Leviatan, bestow upon me the strength of your force! Let the serpent tell me the lies of my enemies! Allow my empathy to be my protection! Allow my anger to be swift with justice! Be present that our enemies will not conquer us! I offer requests of healing and emotional balance that I may employ your creation to do so! Hail Leviatan. the Dragon of Hell!

CAOSGI CINXIR PERIPSAX, NONCI VOVINA TIAMAT!

I invoke you, Tiamat, Mother of the Abominations of Earth! Dragon of Hell, I invoke you through your ancient names:

UMMU-HUBUR, TEHOM, VOVIN, TANNIN, LEVIATAN TIAMAT!

I CALL YOU FORTH TO ENTER MY BEING QUEEN OF GODS, MOTHER OF DEMONS! COME FORTH FROM THE UNDERWORLD REALM OF THAUMIEL, SURROUND ME WITH SHADOWS OF THE LIGHT AND THE LIGHT FROM THE SHADOWS!

PRIMAL DRACONIAN GODDESS, TIAMAT, CROWN ME AS AN ANCIENT ONE!

BUSDIR A TIAMAT!

INVOCATION OF AZAZEL

EYA ON CA AZAZEL AKEN!

ITZREL ITZREL AZAZEL! (x3)

AZAZEL, I INVOKE THEE BY THE ANCIENT WORDS KNOWN BY THY TRUE WORSHIPERS!

HAIL TO AZAZEL, THE PRIDEFUL SCAPEGOAT, WHO RISETH FORTH FROM THE PITS OF HELL! LEND ME YOUR DIVINE WISDOM THAT I MAY GAIN POWER AND THE TREASURES YOU POSSESS! LORD OF THE NEPHILIM! MAJESTIC GOAT, DESERT DJINN, MIGHTY AZAZEL! TAL SHATA ALSI-KUTU, TOLA SHUTA LAM-ASKE! HEAR NOW THE COVENANT OF IBLIS AND THE DARK LORDS OF THE ABYSS! LORD AZAZEL, ATTEND THIS RITE AND FILL ME WITH THE GNOSIS OF THE BLACK GOAT! LORD AZAZEL, SHEPHERD OF THE SATANIC GOAT, COME FORTH AND MANIFEST THYSELF! BESTOW THE BLESSINGS OF HELL UPON ME! RISE BEFORE ME, FOUL FIEND OF THE INFERNO! I CALL AND CONJURE THEE FORTH TO STAND WITH ME IN THIS TEMPLE! I SUMMON YOU TO APPEAR BEFORE ME IN A FORM YOU SO DESIRE AND COMMUNICATE WITH ME!

AZAZEL, THE NEPHILIM KNOWN AS AZAZYEL, ENTER THIS BODY AND FORTIFY IT WITH YOUR ESSENCE!

APERIATUR DUDAEL, ET GERMINET AZAZEL!

INVOCATION OF ASMODEUS/SAMAEL

EIDOS EIDOS TEIFRAS ABUA TLINX!

ECCE CALICEM VENERO, SAMAEL!

FALLEN ANGEL SAMAEL ASHMEDAI, HEAR MY CALLING AND COME TO MY TEMPLE OF FLESH!

SHEMNA'IL, NASIRU'D-DIN, ASHMEDAI, CHAVAYOTH, SAKLAS, SAMAEL!

COME FORTH TO ME, MANIFEST IN MY BEING SO WE CAN JOIN AS ONE! SERPENT OF ELDER POWERS, GREAT FATHER OF CAIN, COME FROM YOUR REALM OF SITRA AHRA AND BESTOW YOUR BLESSINGS UPON ME! DARK ONE OF THE DEEP, EVIL RULER OF THE QLIPHOTH!

EL NESHIAH SCAN TSEBEL ESPHOR NOCTARAK EDATUR NONZITRAEL VACAZAZOCH HE NEBESUSHTAR STEL NESBAIN SLUU AMEL ELERTU SFAGN ESPHAMAS ASBENIT VENAR SEBETH SATASHTEL INNON CAAMON VELROHET!

I INVOKE THEE, SAMAEL, HORNED ONE, THE SERPENT OF THE DEEP! COME TO ME SAMAEL AND REVEAL TO ME THE NATURE OF DEMONS!

ANANEL! ABRADAHABRA! ADIRO-ADISANA!

Venomous God, make me into a black magic adept and a wise person.

SAMAEL, RAAL SHEYL 'ELOHIM, LAVO L'TOKH' HABASHO'AR SHEYLI!

All glory be to Samael!

Ayer avage Aloren Asmodeus aken!

I call to thee, Asmodai, who is also revered as Samael, Poison of God, King of the Demons! Lord over all those who practice the dark arts! Teach me the ways of Sorcery and the art of poetry! I need your help Asmodeus, give me thy secrets!

Ayer avage Aloren Asmodeus aken!(x2)

Demon of Lust, Jealousy, Anger and Revenge, I seek the many realms of pleasure! Chief Astrologer of Hell, you ride upon the back of a dragon and you breathe fire! Fire-breathing Asmodeus, I call to you!

Ayer avage Aloren Asmodeus aken!(x3)

You spread the wickedness of man! You have knowledge of the future! You have angel wings and the tail of a serpent! One of the most evil of Satan's infernal Demons, I call you, Asmodeus, Supreme Master of the Nine Hells! Great King, Strong and Powerful, who sits upon the back of a dragon in flames! Asmodeus, with the heads of a bull, a man, and a ram, show me the places where you hide your treasures!

SELOR ZETASTU VOTR KENEB TESEABON

KL ATONOA NINGEL VARANTAR YATATUR BABANNIM KATABESH SORONOROS!

Asmodeus, I call to thee!

Come forth, Asmodeus, within this body which I have prepared!

Come forth, Samael Asmodai, and enter my flesh!

The gate is open!

SAMAEL ASHMEDAI, ANI KORE LEKH L'TOKH HAGUF SHEYLI!

Drink from Chalice

Sum Harba de Asmodai Malka!

Ave colligare Asmodai!

Invocation of Astarot

Tasa alora foren Astarot!(x3)

Ishtar, Astarte, Inanna, Isis, Tanit-Ashtart, Astarot! Queen of Vipers, I call to thee to come to my temple and manifest! Hail Astarot! Great Princess of Love and War! Bringer of the Twilight; O mighty Viper of love's burning desire. I humbly invoke You, O Queen of Heaven; I invite you to come forth from the sky, to come forth from the ends of the earth and to come forth from the depths of the underworld. Hear my prayer oh blessed , and greet me as your servant and friend! I wish only to get to know You, and to rejoice in the fiery light of your

MAJESTIC SPIRIT.

GRAND DUKE OF THE WESTERN REGIONS OF HELL, SATAN'S DAUGHTER, I INVOKE THEE, COME TO ME!

YA NUCAR ZFON ISMALOS GHOSH AYNZUMEIN TEITOSHURAR ANACIS TLEX ZERABTU SCIMMEBELIAYAZN VTA AKL ESPHAMEN AZ NUCILTOR VAZITER NENZOTM TLAF KARONASH EMERTU XENOBAS UTTAR NENEB VA ILZEBETH YAVONESH HE!

INVOCATION OF BELZEBUD

ADEY VOCAR AVAGE BELZEBUD! (x3)

BELZEBUD, LORD OF EVERYTHING THAT FLIES, I DO INVOKE YOU BY YOUR ANCIENT NAMES:

BEELZEBUTH, ENLIL, BAAL ZEBUL, BEL, BEELZEBUB, BELZEBUD!

HAIL BELZEBUD, GOD OF THE PHILISTINES! THE SECOND IN COMMAND, I DEMAND THAT YOU FILL ME WITH YOUR BLACK ESSENCE, INFECT MY MIND WITH YOUR VOICE, AND PREPARE MY SOUL FOR GODHOOD. PRINCE OF THE SERAPHIM AND PRINCE OF THE AIR, I DECLARE THAT YOU ARE SOVEREIGN AND UNIQUE IN WISDOM! BELZEBUD, COME FORTH AND MANIFEST THYSELF WITHIN THIS BODY AS A TEMPLE IN WHICH I HAVE PREPARED!

BELZEBUD, LORD OF THE FLIES, ENTER MY SOUL, SHOW ME THE OTHER SIDE, AND OPEN MY EYES THAT I MAY SEE THE DARK RECESSES OF HELL. I IMPLORE YOU THAT YOU TAKE MY HAND AND GUIDE ME THROUGH THE PATHWAYS OF THE VOID! GOD OF STORMS, I INVITE YOU TO COME TO ME AND SHOW ME THE SECRETS OF THE DARK ORACLE. MASTER OF THE ZODIAC, TEACH ME THY WAYS, GIVE ME THE POWER

OVER ALL THAT FLIES. ENDOW ME WITH EXTRAORDINARY POWER AND AUTHORITY! BAAL ZEBUL, LORD OF THE HIGH HOUSE, LORD OF THE NORTH, I CALL TO YOU.

ABEA SKL NERRAZATAF SHOKMAEL BEATAS IN CARNEBIS MAZMIZEIM ETER ARTA, ARTA SCAMO BEBELOS VO ERIT ! ABILSA ZEIDA NOTTERIAH AMISCATON TETEAB ANOPHRIS GAADAAT ECHINOCH! ZEIDA ZEIDA LAMMOS KTAN!

BAAL ZEBUL KOSED IK ESSET TELOK!

Invocation of the Forces of Darkness

ACTATOS, CATIPTA, BEJOURAN, ITAPAN, MARNUTUS!

ACTEUS, MAGELSIUS, ORMENUS, LYCAS, NICON, MIMON!

I INVOKE THE FORCES OF DARKNESS THAT RULE OVER THE QLIPHOTH!

LIFTOACH KLIFFOT!

MAY THE WISDOM, POWER, AND IMMORTALITY OF MY MIND ALWAYS SEEK SELF-EXCELLENCE! SAMAEL ASHMEDAI, THE BLACK POISON OF GOD, MAY WORK WITH MY WISDOM AND keep me focused on my path of self-deification! Satan bless my work that I may ascend alone and powerful! Almighty and Ineffable Lord Samyaza, our Master Lucifer, the Prince of Darkness.

Palas Aron Ozinomas Baske Bano Tudan Donas Geheamel Cla Orlay Berec He Pantaras Tay!

I invoke and harness all the demonic energy possible in the world, I harness all the Forces of Darkness to follow my will. I invite the Forces of Darkness to bestow their infernal power upon me!

May my Father, the Devil, give me the strength of the Black Flame which I can use to the best of my advantage!

ATAZOT!

Invocation of Lilith

Renich viasa avage Lilith lirach!

I invoke you, Black Goddess Lilith! Consort of Lucifer and Asmodeus, heed the call and come to me!

Marag Ama Lilith Rimok Samalo Naamah! (x13)

Lilith, Mother of Demons, Queen of Vampires, Ruler of Harlots, Empress of Evil and the Bride of Lucifer, come to me from your realm in Gamaliel and fill my mind, body and soul with your essence! Sister of Agrat, Mahalath, and Naamah who rules the Qliphoth as Queen!

Lilith, Queen of the Night, come to my temple of

flesh! Appear before me, Mother of Evil Demons! Make me into your demonic child!

Fac mecum est in utero habens de Spiritu Draco!

It is my Will to invoke the spirit of Lilith, so that by her spirit, I experience the power of the Bringer of Death to obtain her Words of Power!

    ANI OHEVET OTAKH AMA LEYLIT!

OEOS ACAPHOSH NYOT ZELESH ISTVAMAN TENEB NSGIAH ATOMOR NE AMMITABAS NORZEBR EYATTAN KELOSH TSABELMES NRIOZT HANANEF FTAA EOS GHAT!

LEYLIT, ANI HAYAL'DAH SHEL'KHA!

Black Moon, Lilith, whose brood are all the demons that roam the Earth, mold me as clay from fire. Blood Red Moon, Lilith, Queen of the Night, take the flight! Speak the words of power and reveal to me the Gnosis of Truth!

In the presence of dark, nameless, and formless gods, may my true will open the gates of the dark Gamaliel and make contact with the hellish Demon Queen and Mother Lilith.

    May the Mystery of the Qliphoth open tonight in the name of Lucifer!

    Hail Lilith!

Invocation of Naamah

NIBES VA ESTER NEMETT SCAMMON TZETALARON SEHENECH NUTAR ZEBELTU TSATSHATR EZARABAH VATRISH XALA XALA EA STORR NEBIS!

Naamah, Princess of Screeching, Lady of the Gate, I invoke you!

Demon Queen, Bride of Samael Asmodai, Lady of the Earth, I implore you to bestow pleasures and riches upon me! You are the Woman of Midnight and the Fount of All Sorcery!

NAAMAH, L'HAFUKH OTIY LA'ELOHIM!

Naamah, sister of Lilith, do come forth! Queen of Nehemoth, enter my temple of flesh! Appear Mother of Darkness! It is you who bewitches men and leads them to infernal eternity! Mistress of Death, fill me with the terrors of the night and seize me with temptation!

NAAMAH, ANI OHEVET OTAKH!

Queen of Nehemoth, enter my flesh and inflame my soul with your essence!

NAAMAH, BO EYLI!

Invocation of Hecate

Anana Hecate ayer!

I invoke Thee, Hecate, Queen of Sorcery! Goddess of the Crossroads of Hell, hear my prayer and come to me! Bestow your blessings upon me and my soul. Queen of all Witchcraft, your path is as black as night! I invoke you through your ancient names:

Phosphoros, Soteira, Propolos, Trioditis, Artemis, Hecate!

Queen of Shadows, you lead the soul into the Underworld to find wisdom of the Gods of Old, so that men may travel into the heart of the Infernal Empire.

Salve Luna Infortuna Nocticula Hecate!

Hecate Romerac, Liftoach Kliffoth! Solstitii Temporis Sensvs, clarifica me!

Artemis—Hecate, Goddess of Dark Places, I ask that you use your dark alchemy to empower my soul! Come Hecate, come now into this Temple and lay your hand upon me to make me a God! Come! Come now and fill me with your power!

Ave Abnukta Hecate! Ave Nocticula Hecate! Ave Trivia Hecate!

NETATRON CASANAIM ELIS NORMAX EL SOTE DISCON VARAMAR!

Invocation of Set

SA-TA AT-NE-SA!

I invoke Set, the Serpent and the Dragon, the Lord of Egypt, Giver of Life and Bringer of Death, the Egyptian Prince of Darkness, I call you into my mind, body and soul. Your gift is the Black Flame and you're the companion of those who travel the Gates of the Black Sun! You are omniscient, omnipresent and omnipotent! Open the pathways of the Nightside as I invoke you through your ancient names known by Thy true worshipers!

Sutuakh, Typhon, Bolchoseth, Erbeth, Pakerbeth, Set!

Lord of the Desert, son of Satan, he who brings forth darkness of the crimson desert! Set-Heh, the Red One, God of Infinite Future, crown me as a Pharaoh!

Xepera Xeper Xeperu!

Enshroud me with the Powers of Darkness!

IO Erbeth, IO Pakerbeth, IO Bolchoseth, Sutuakh! SA-TA AT-NE-SA!

Lord of Storms, make the magic work by the power of my Will! Sut! Anat! I invoke Thee! Ancient Serpent who holds the keys to the Gnosis of the Black Flame!

Typhon Kolchoi Tontonon Set!

ATARABESH SLUU KERT TE ARTUTAN YA TENARAMAR KHOOS EIAHAOZ REBELSUT NECAFOSH STERB AVENOSH SOKHET NISTAMALOS

ARAI!

Invocation of Cain

Zammazo Emoth Zaraqaen Baaltzelmoth!

I invoke Cain, Tubal-Cain, Camio, the first murderer, I call to you, I invoke you!

Heil Cain von Samael! Ave Cain Messor! Salve Senor la Muerte!

QAYIN FALXIFER + ADIAPHOTOS + QAYIN OCCISOR + MAHAN + QABIL + SENOR DE LA CRUZ NEGRA + QAYIN MORTIFER

Cain, I call you into my mind, my heart and my body! Empower my soul with your divine Sorcery and Alchemy! Spiritual Son of Lucifer and Lilith, I invoke thee!

KAYIN, ANI KORE LEYKH!

Invocation of Molok

Molok, Twin God of Satan!

Arise! Move and Appear!

I invoke you through your ancient names:

Milcom, Molekh, Malkam, Malik, Makkal, Moloch!

Zodacare od Zodameranu!

I am the Lord of light and darkness as separate! I am the One that rules the transformation of the self into whatever one chooses to be! I am the Lord and Keeper of the Black Diamond! I am the king of death and life! I am the lord of the one they call the Higher Self! I am the God of the Underworld! I am the Great Prince of the Black Sun! I am the Dark Twin Molok, and I rule over the realm of Thaumiel along with Satan!

Invocation of Adramelech

Aperiatur Acharayim, et germinet Adramelech!

I call upon Adramelech, Grand Chancellor, President of Satan's General Council, to come to my temple and manifest! Liftoach Kliffot!

Great art of words is thy greatest inspiration!

Infernal Peacock King of the Forbidden Qliphothic Sphere, I ask thy gate to open! Your name is Adra-Malik, the King of Poison! Agios Adramelech Rex Venenum!

God of the Avites, the enemy of God, President of the High Council of Devils, I call to you!

    LEPACA SAMAEL SEMELIN ADRAMELECH RUACH GONOGIN!

Invocation of Ninnghizhidda

    ALSI KU NUSHI, DINGIR NINNGHIZHIDDA, MUSH-SHA-TUR INA ZU-AB!

I invoke Ninnghizhidda, the Horned Serpent of the Deep, Watcher of the Gate of Ganzir, the Hellish Pit! You are the Horned Snake which I dream of awake! In the name of our Father Satan, Lord and Master of all Magicians, open the Gate that I may enter! Demon of Enki, I call you into my being. Fill me with the power over the dead! I invoke you through your ancient names:

    Thoth, Tehuti, Hermes, Mercury, Quetzalcoatl, Ninnghizhidda!

    ALSI KU NUSHI SIR ZU-AB NINNGHIZHIDDA!

Invocation of Nyarlathotep

Samak daram surabel karameka amuranas Ekotos mirat-fortin ranerug + Dalerinter marban porafin + Herikoramonus derogex + Iratisinger!

Ia Nyarlathotep! Great Messenger, Father of the Million Favored Ones! Bringer of Joy throughout the Void! Hail the Black Pharaoh and stalker among the weak! I praise thee, faceless and wandering one! Enter this temple and fill me with your essence so I can have dreams in the witch house! Each pact I've made with you has brought me closer and closer to you, jet-black humanoid of madness, the Black Man of the Witch's Sabbat!

Ia Nyarlathotep! Zi kia kanpa! Zi anna kanpa! Ia ia Nyarlathotep! Zi dingir kia kanpa! Zi dingir anna kanpa! Nyarlathotep kanpa! Ia Nyarlathotep gal dingir, ensi dingir! Glestju zu zagmi, glestju zu gala! Alka Nyarlathotep! Maharu anu sharaku alka, emqu Nyarlathotep gal di ak Kadath! Ir zu sharaku gjestju gju nam sjita silim, alka Nyarlathotep zi dingir kia kanpa! Zi dingir anna kanpa! Kakammu – kakammu – kakammu! Samak daram surabel karameka amuranas + Sedhi + Ihdes + Doros Serod!

Invocation of the Antichrist Spirit Mabus

RIPTAL VRAGD KIBRAGIDA VRIAM ZIGAZ GISMILA ARAL KRIVA AR ZHARAK ATIDOR HORIGME ARDIT KAR ASLA PHER O EA NIPHUZ ZET ZEA IN KRIDYULTH ZRAG LA GRIAR IFRAK VIZRALAR BHAGIM HILBLAR VAZOE ADIN GILART ZAAR ZLARTAR AREOR AYAZIN KUVKLA KAIN VIGIGI ZIMIRRO EA UR!

I am the Antichrist, the true Anointed One, the Messiah of Satanists and Luciferians alike!

I am the son of Satan Incarnate! I am the Beast! I am the Man of Sin! I am the Lawless One! I am the King of the World!

I summon and invoke you ruler of chaos.

I who am of True Gothic Spirit call forth and summon you to embrace and guide me! I, your unholy vessel, conjure thee forth from this sacred space! Hear my voice and smell thy incense! Destroy my enemies and shower upon them your power of the Devil!

Chapter 7: Evocations

Conjuration of Lucifer

Emperor Lucifer, whom I call the mighty Lord Satan, Prince and Master of the rebellious spirits, condescend to be favorable — so it shall be!
Ruler of Thaumiel, the almighty and ineffable god Satan Lucifer, I implore you to abandon your dwelling to come speak with me!

Liftoach shaari ha-Thaumiel B'Shem ha-Satan va-Molok! (x11)

Lucifer, Ouia, Kameron, Aliseon, Mandesumini, Poemi, Oriet, Naydrus, Parinoscon, Eparinesoni, Estiot, Dumoson, Divorcon, Danokar, Casmiel, Hayras, Hugras, Fabelleronthon, Uli, Sodierno, Petan!

Come Lucifer, come! I invite you to come forth!

Conjuration of Baphomet

Baphomet! Illuminati Goat God of Darkness, Light and Liberation! I call you forth to manifest thyself to me in a form you so desire that will be recognizable! I invoke thee! I conjure thee! Come forth to me! Zirlat Ramadan Ziram! As above, so below; black and white; good and evil; darkness and light! I ask you to manifest yourself to me! I call you forth to enter my being God of the Light, Baphomet, Great Architect of the Universe, Baphomet, I call thee forth! (x3)

Conjuration of Belzebud

I implore you Belzebud, Lord over All that Flies, to come to this temple and manifest! Belzebud, Lucifer, Madilon, Salimo, Sarai, Theu, Ameklo, Saugriel, Prarebud, Adricanorom, Marteino, Timo, Kameron, Forsei, Metosite, Prumosy, Dumaso, Elivisa, Alfris, Fubentroty! Come Belzebud, come! (x3)

Conjuration of Astarot

I implore you, Astarot, the Western Crowned Princess of Hell, to come to my temple and manifest!

Astarot, Ador, Cemaso, Valuerituf, Mareso, Lodir, Cadomir, Aluiel, Calniso, Tely, Plirom, Viordy, Cureviorbas, Cameron, Vesturiel, Vulnavij, Benez meus Calmiron, Noard, Nisa Kenibrano Calvodium, Broza Tabrasil! Come Astarot, come! I invite you into my mind and body! (x3)

Conjuration of Azazel

I invite you to come forth Azazel, Master of the Dark Arts! I implore you to come to my temple and manifest! Son of Satan, come to me by the words that follow:

Osurmi, Delmuson, Atalami, Karushon, Melani, Liamintho, Colehon, Paron, Madon, Baninel, Vermisa, Sluroa, Nolema, Dorsemat, Lavala, Omor, Frangom, Balder, Drakon, Come Azazel, come now! I invite you to this sacred space! (x3)

Conjuration of Belial

King Belial, Ruler of the Earth, Lord of the North, open the gates to the passage of Bohu and reveal The Black Diamond! RA SHA BELIAL, Darmusin, Parinobohu, Atalki, Nolamar, Nolami, Amar, Matos, Lamava, Culedom, Osurmi, Frangom, Balder, Drakon! Enter my flesh Beliar! I implore you to enter my dwelling and come socialize with me!

Conjuration of Tiamat/Leviatan

Tiamat! Leviatan! Drakon! Lotan! Tehom! Theli! Tannin!
I conjure forth the Dragon of the Earth, the Serpent of the Void, the Worm of Chaos and Monster of Thaumiel! May Leviatan be the Serpent of Timeless Existence who comes to me as the key to all knowledge and power! Tiamat—Leviatan, the Water Ruler of the West who is favored by Satan! I implore you to abandon the world of darkness to enter my realm of light! Ancient Demoness of Atlantis who is the gate to the hidden gnosis and power of my soul, I call you forth! I implore you to come forth to grant me the wisdom of dark souls!

VOVIN! (x6)

I conjure up the Chaos Dragon of the Ancient Ones and Great Old Ones who are Sumerian and Chaldean in origin, but also from the Necronomicon Book of Dead Names! IA TIAMAT! Hail Leviatan, the Dragon of the Deep, the Lord of Ancient Sumeria and Babylon! Erim, the Great Serpent of Gothic Chaos, I invoke your power, I invoke your presence! Come Tiamat, come! I invite you to come forth into this sacred space in which I hath prepared in this moment!

Conjuration of Samael

Asmodeus, the great Fallen Angel of Poison who is Samael, do come forth! I invite you into this sacred space to accompany me in my Magic! I conjure the Power of the Samael, the Black, Poison of God, thy great Asmodai, the Devil who rules Golachab and is an Ancient One, the second consort of Lilith who is of Demons and Dark Spirits, I invoke your sacred presence in this Ritual of Illumination and Sorcery! Hail the one adorned with fire!

LARAD HA-SHAYAT MOVET DOREGES ASMODAI!

Conjuration of Lilith

(For this Conjuration, you will need a red apple, a chalice filled with wine with a few drops of blood, a prayer to burn in the flame of a black candle, and a Wand)

1.) Write the following prayer with Dragon's Blood Ink on a clean and blank piece of paper, preferably parchment paper:

"LAMIA + MINO + PALIFASTA + DEMECHA + HAIM + FIRMIS

I invite you to come forth Lilith! Come, bestow upon me your presence Lilitu! Black Goddess of the Moon, I call to you! Sinful Witch, Mother of Demons, Lucifer's Consort! In the name of the Dragon, bless me with your company!"

2.) Conduct a ritual by reading aloud the

handwritten prayer and burning it in the flame of a black candle.

3.) Holding the Wand, recite the following:

Marag Ama Lilith Rimok Samalo Naamah! (x13)

Renich viasa avage Lilith lirach! (x4)

Agrat Mahalath Taninsam Ama Lilith, Liftoach Kliffot! (x2)

Woman of the Black Moon, Lilith, the Queen of Hell, Vampire Queen of Gamaliel, I conjure thee forth!

Eat the apple or at least take a few bites of it

HAIL LILITH!

4.) After finishing the ritual, meditate, paying attention to anything that goes on, such as hearing Lilith communicate.

Incantations to Summon Evil Spirit

O Lama + Basulai + Monai + Mempis + Lorrate + Pacem!

*After the spirit manifests in any way, recite the following Greeting to All Spirits to welcome him/her/them:

Palifasta + Firmis + Demecha + Haim!

Oh, Evil Spirit of Satan who I've summoned, I implore you to grant me thy blessing!

Conjuration of the Black Flame

I conjure and summon the Black Flame that burns within me brightly. The Eternal Fire which inflames me deep within my being. I evoke the Essence of Sitra Ahra, the Qliphothic Realms which I conjure to consume my visionaries of this evil mundane world that I so happen to hate. Spirit of the Abyss, the Wrecker of Blackness, Guardian of Darkness, Lord of Truth, come forth and withstand me within these Lands of Evil! Divine Spirit of the Black Flame, blazing like a torch that can't be extinguished! Come forth in this body which I hath prepared for communion. Come to me!

Regnum Luciferi Excelsi! Potens serpens Satanas, diabolicum spiritum tuum de me matum et serve quia ego sum. Imperatoris Lucifer, princeps ac dominus de spirituum rebellum deficientium, quaeso te.

Prescio + Mipot + Domisiac + Tufi + Maha + Huschia + Laemelisete + Hedera + Cade + Veleadis + Locisomnibus + Amesiamin + Ariorosh + Laedemische + Jehonale + Jehonale + Hisipo + Hisanam + Podarasche + Podarasche! Palifasta + Firmis + Demecha + Haim! Zarlat Ramadan Ziram!

NAMAKLA CHISRA DEUS ETEREM SALIBAT CRAEUMSLE! DRAKON NIMON!

Conjuration of a Djinn

(NAME OF DJINN SAID 21 TIMES)

I summon forth (NAME OF DJINN) from darkest pits of the Black Earth to be present before me! I call out to the ancient spirit of the smokeless fire! May you serve your Unholy Father Iblis the Shaitan forevermore and manifest within the magic summoning space! (Djinn's Name Three Times) come forth! Come forth (Djinn's Name) and fill this temple with your dark presence! I summon you forth from the wastelands! I summon you forth from the Underworld! Hear my voice beckon and come thou forth!

I call you forth (Djinn's Name) from the smokeless fire! (x6)

Conjuration of Iblis the Shaitan

Iblis! Devil Man of the Dark, Opposer of all things good in the World, I call you forth from your dwelling in whichever part of the world you are in to come here so I can see you! Shaitan, smell my incense burning within this temple! Shaitan, hear my voice beckon! Come forth Ifris and see my candles burn brightly as I ask you to manifest thy ancient Chief of the Desert Djinn! I summon the fire of Al—Iblis! Come to me so I can accept you as my Master! All Hail Iblis the Shaitan! (x3)

How to Respectfully Summon a Demon

Write down the following prayer on a clean piece of paper:

"Emperor Lucifer, by your grace, grant me the power to conceive in my mind a Spirit of Evil under your command. In nomine Draco, quo veniat satanas Lucifer! I humbly and respectfully ask you in your name that (NAME OF DEMON) will manifest before me, that he/she will give me a faithful and true answer so that I may accomplish my desires. May my endeavors be fulfilled and wishes be granted in accordance with the chosen Goetic Demon of my choice. LEMON SESEL NIDAR HORIEL PEUNT + HALMON + BANIEL + VERMIAS + SLEVOR + NOELMA + DORSAMOT + LHAVALA + OMOR + FRAMGAM + BELDOR + DRAKON + Come (NAME OF SPIRIT)"

When you're finished writing the prayer, you have to conduct a Standard Ritual burning the prayer in the flame of the required colored candle of the Demon. Meditate on the energies presented to you in the ritual of the Demon, and you may actually see it.

You must know the reason and purpose you summon the Demon. You also must know what to give back in return.

Chapter 8: Incantations to Open the Gates of Hell

Below are Incantations given to me by the Devil himself to Open the Gates of Hell, which are the Chakras of course! Recite each phrase 11 times and meditate for 30 minutes for each incantation. Be careful, these incantations are powerful and can summon evil spirits that can torment those who are without!

1.) Chant to Open the Third Eye and Sixth Chakra:
NOKTALAK NANNA EUMRA TALAS MIKMA! (x11)
"Let me see what can't be seen Nanna!"

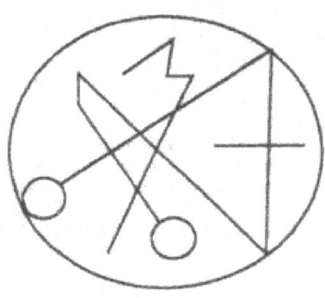

**2.) CHANT TO OPEN THE CROWN CHAKRA:
RAMAS MARDUK ANDAR, ENHAL THULAK
ENIKAR! (x11)**

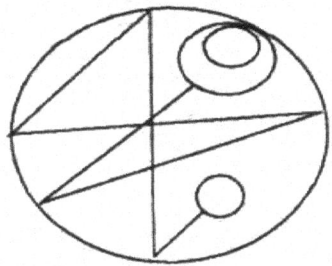

"BY THE POWER OF MARDUK, MAY WISDOM FALL FROM ABOVE!"

**3.) CHANT TO OPEN THE THROAT CHAKRA:
AZAZAZA THUL GHARNA NEBO! (x11)**
"I CREATE WHAT I SPEAK WITH NEBO'S MAGIC!"

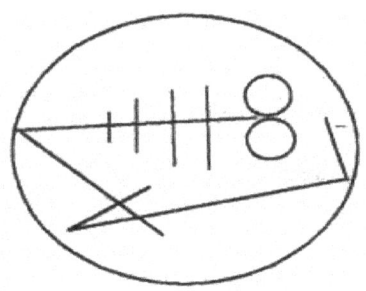

**4.) CHANT TO OPEN THE HEART CHAKRA:
INANNA GERAM AT UL THIAM! (x11)
"INANNA ONLY LOVES THE FALLEN ONES!**

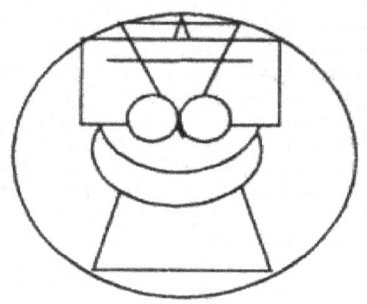

**5.) CHANT TO OPEN THE SOLAR PLEXUS CHAKRA:
SAGBA DINGIR SHAMMASH, KIA KANPA!
(x11)**

"UNHOLY SPIRIT SHAMMASH, EARTH REMEMBERS"

6.) CHANT TO OPEN THE SACRAL CHAKRA:
NERGAL KANDAR TRUS DEMATOS! (x11)
"NERGAL'S GATE OF HELL, OPEN!"

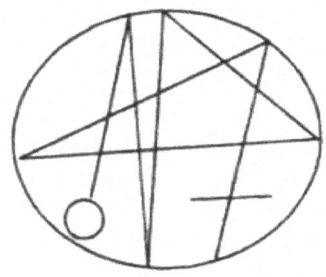

7.) CHANT TO OPEN THE ROOT CHAKRA:
NINIB KIAK SA ZOVAS INFERNI! (x11)
"NINIB OPEN THE GATE OF THE INFERNO!"

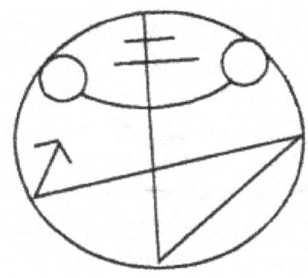

Chapter 9: Power Meditation

As a Luciferian, it is very important to meditate during and after each ritual. In Luciferian Sorcery, meditation is what opens the soul, your psychic senses and your chakras, which is a form of divinity. You must meditate at least 15 minutes per day if you want to have godlike power. Before I started Luciferianism, I was a Spiritual Satanist and I was taught that I had to meditate in the Sun to increase my bioelectricity throughout my body and with increased bioelectricity, you can do a lot of stuff you never knew you had in you. I had a conflict one time in college when a friend came up to me and told me one of our classmates called her fat, so I telepathically communicated with Lucifer himself asking him if I could do some magic on the offender to teach her a lesson and Lucifer agreed. So in the middle of class, I stared her down and waved my fingers in a sort of pentagram in the air and somehow ants appeared on the seat next to her. The powers of the mind and soul are very real. You can do just about anything after a long time of meditating. Going a long time meditating then stopping for a few days will only make you behind what you can actually manifest in this world. Since Lucifer is God of this World, he gives us his alchemical gold from the Sun to transform us in the Dragon's Fire.

There's something important to realize in this big picture. You must do a pact with Lucifer in order to have godlike powers. This is also known as dedicating your soul to Satan. A lot of occultists say Satan and Lucifer are not the same, but he is to me. He is the Emperor of the Infernal Empire and he is the most powerful deity. It's through a pact with Lucifer that we receive Lucifer's gnosis, power and gifts. I will go more into a pact with Lucifer later in the book, but right now I'm going to talk about the most important meditations you can do.

Sun Meditation

For this meditation, you have to sit cross-legged facing the Sun. Imagine a white gold energy radiating with your eyes closed.

Vibrate, "R-A-U-M" with one long exhale, then breathe in again. Do this 23 times. You will notice you have a good charge of energy.

You must visualize the Sunshine entering your body and transforming your soul. This is the basic meditation I use daily.

Draconian Flame Meditation

Stare at a red candle and visualize the flame getting bigger and brighter to the point where it almost engulfs you. Make the flame big enough to where you can see it with your eyes closed. Imagine the flame expanding to where it touches your aura. Now say, "I invoke the Dragon's Fire, the Black Flame of Lucifer."

Now visualize the flame catching your astral body on fire. You burn with the glory of Luciferian Light. Keep doing this meditation for around 15 minutes and you will feel rejuvenated and relaxed afterwords.

Luciferian Light Meditation

Sit in a comfortable spot, relax, and go into a meditative state. Now, visulaize your astral body growing bigger and brighter with your aura expanding, doing this for five minutes. With a long breath out, vibrate, "NONASTURMA DAY EVA AMERI TAT, USHU ANAR ASTA."

Do this meditation for around 30 minutes every day and you will notice a big change in how your aura appears to people.

These three meditations are just a few examples of the types of meditations you can do. You can use other mantras to meditate on, just as long as you have an idea.

Chapter 10: Spells and Sigils to Manifest Desires

These sigils are to be made with a written prayer relating to the affirmation below the specific sigil.

FOR EXAMPLE:

"I AM THE WITCH OF SMOKE AND FLAME. I SEEK THE SECRETS OF FORGOTTEN GNOSIS AND SORCERY. MAY THE LADY OF THE CROOKED PATH, HECATE, GUIDE ME THROUGH THE MYSTERIES OF THE CRAFT! EXAT!"

"EXAT" IS QLIPHOTHIC WORD WHICH TRANSLATES TO "LET IT BE THUS!"

THE MORE SOMEONE RHYMES USING WORDS OF POWER AND THE FOCUS ON INTENT IS WHAT DETERMINES HOW POWERFUL YOUR SPELL WILL BE.

HERE IS A PHRASE I USE TO INSTANTLY MANIFEST MY DESIRES:

ARTABA USSA MANUKMA DARNA KANDU STRATA

THE AVOVE AFFIRMATIONS ARE EXAMPLES OF HOW A SPELL SHOULD BE MADE. THE SORCERER OR SORCERESS SHOULD CREATE THE SIGIL AND A POSITIVE AFFIRMATION FOR THAT SIGIL, THEN WRITE OUT AN APPROPRIATE PRAYER FOR THE SEAL, BURNING IT IN THE FLAME OF AN APPROPRIATE CANDLE. THAT IS HOW MY SPELLS ARE DONE FOR THE MOST PART. YOU CAN USE THE SIGILS ON THE PREVIOUS PAGE IF YOU WANT, OR YOU CAN CREATE YOUR OWN. I RECOMMEND YOU CREATE YOUR OWN, BECAUSE THAT MAKES THE SPELL MORE POWERFUL.

Spell to Become a Demon

Requirements:

- Parchment paper
- Dragon's Blood ink
- quirell or calligraphy pen
- Dragon's Blood and Musk incense
- a doll that represents you made out of either cloth or something else that's flammable to be soaked in the fluids
- your own hair
- your own blood
- your fingernails (optional)
- a red and/or black candle
- your Wand
- a silver burning bowl

This is a fun and easy spell to do. First, take a piece of parchment paper and use the quirell and Dragon's Blood ink to create your own demonic sigil, then cover it with your blood, hair and fingernails. This is the sigil I created that was given to me by Satan:

 <-- The Sigil of Mabus

After you create your sigil using the Dragon's Blood ink, turn around the dried sigil to where it's from top to bottom, but laid on its back so you can write out the following prayer:

"Satan, grant me thy blessing! Transform me into a child of the Dragon of Fire! Your son/daughter I wish to be, requesting that you make me anew as a demon, a teacher and a demigod of those who wish to become! I desire to be more like you, ruling the world as my own God among men! I will create a kingdom on Earth and rule it as a King/Queen, to be without a superior, forever cursing those who stand in my way! I won't disappoint you my Dark Lord! Master, grant me the gift of the Black Flame!"

Once the other side of the parchment paper has dried, make sure one side of the paper contains your sigil and the other side contains the prayer. Now, this is important: after reading out your prayer containing your self-created demonic sigil. Burn the Sigil/Prayer in the flame of the red or black candle, reciting the following words of power:

"KIL-LA-KE! RAMASTA! SHADIAH!"

Make sure the ashes get on a plate or some kind of flat surface you can easily dust off the ashes from. Collect the ashes and put them in a glass jar that has your blood, saliva and urine in it.

Keep the jar covered outside for 3 days under the Sun and Moon. Take the jar after 3 days and conduct a ritual.

First, begin by calling the four quarters:

 East — Lucifer
North — Belzebud
 West — Tiamat
 South — Azazel

After you have invoked each Deity, recite the following:

  I, (N.N.), a child of Satan, do hereby on this day of (DATE) do wish to become a Fallen Angel Demonic Spirit of Old! If this is granted for me, I promise I will forever be in the service of Lucifer, my Infernal Master.

 Put some of your blood on your sigil and into the jar

By the names of Lucifer, Belzebud, Tiamat and

Azazel, I am now a child of the Dragon and a Demon of Satan! I forever hold the keys to the Knowledge of the Ancients and Powers of the Infernal Spirits!"

Take the jar and pour it all on a doll of some sort that represents you inside the silver burning bowl.

Close with a big "Hail Lucifer!"
Congratulations, you're now a Fallen Angel Spirit! See how easy that was?

Chapter 11: The Infernal Spirits

I have 9 main patron Demons. They are Satan Lucifer, Lilith, Azazel, Belial, Leviatan/Tiamat, Hecate, Asmodeus/Samael, Astarot and Nyarlathotep. These Qliphothic Demons are very powerful and are not to be reckoned with if not taken seriously. Always show respect when dealing with these entities. Don't use traditional magic circles, because they are kinda pointless. The only kind of magic circle you should use is Asenath Mason's Qliphothic Magic Circle. These Demons are known by many other names. Lucifer, the most powerful of all the fallen angels for example, is also known as Baphomet, Enki and Satan. Lilith is Lucifer's favorite wife and mother of all Demons. Leviatan, or Tiamat, is the Dragon of the Void, the Serpent of Chaos. Belial and Asmodeus are the two most powerful Demon Kings. Azazel is the son of Satan and is skilled in black magic and warfare. Hecate is Queen of all Witchcraft. Nyarlathotep is the Great Old Messenger of the Necronomicon. All these Demons have various different powers to them and will help you in your ascent, especially Lucifer, because he makes the best teacher.

These are the 9 Demons I like to work with:

Lucifer

Lucifer is the Adversary of the Christian tradition. He has many different forms and appears in many different ways to people. In Luciferianism, we encounter him as the Emperor of Hell Satan, which is his form that predates Christian legends and stories and has nothing to do with the Christian image of the spirit of evil. He is the fallen angel who was cast down for the sin of pride. He is also known as Enki, but also Nyarlathotep of the Necronomicon. In Qabalistic terms, he is associated with the hidden Sephira Daath, which descended to the level of man, awakening the forbidden power of creation and sexual energy. In the Qabalah, the fallen angels and their sexual union with man initiates the union of worlds and opens the forbidden path of soul ascension.

In old grimoires, Lucifer is the Infernal Emperor and Ruler of Hell presiding over the entire Infernal Hierarchy. In traditional demonology, he rules over the element of air and the direction of East. In the Faustian Tradition, he is the chief Ruler of Hell. Lucifer is also the Top Leader of the Nordic Gods of the Empire of Orion, the MOST POWERFUL of all Gods!

Lilith

Lilith is the Mother of Demons and it is within her that the magician must seek the other Qliphoth. It is toward her that the magical pentagram is pointing. The pentagram of dark magic points toward the earth, the soil, toward ancient times and the primordial. It is here that one finds the Qliphoth. The Qliphoth are the reality that we refuse to see. A dark magician does not, like the adept of the light tradition stare up at the heavens in search of some heavenly Utopian world. A dark magician gazes down toward the earth to seek the treasures that have been hidden for thousands of years. The womb of Lilith is the grave that the dark adept freely enters, down into the kingdom of death and the underworld in an initiatory journey towards rebirth.

Animals sacred to Lilith are the owl, serpent and spider. Lilith appears as a night demon in Jewish lore and as a screech owl in Isaiah 34:14 in the King James version of the Bible. In later folklore, "Lilith" is the name for Adam's first wife. She is the first Demoness to be made and she is the first vampire to exist. Samael and Lilith are in the shape of an androgynous being, double-faced, born out of the emanation of the Throne of Glory and corresponding in the spiritual realm to Adam and Eve, who were likewise born as a hermaphrodite. A female demon of the night who supposedly flies around searching for newborn children either to kidnap or strangle them. Also, she sleeps with men to seduce them into propagating demon sons. Legends told about Lilith are ancient. The rabbinical myths of Lilith being Adam's first wife seem to relate to the Sumero-Babylonian Goddess Belit-ili, or Belili. To the Canaanites, Lilith was Baalat, the "Divine Lady." On a tablet from Ur, ca. 2000 BCE, she was addressed as Lillake. Lilith is the Queen of Hell, Demoness of the Night and the Mother of all Demons.

Azazel

Azazel is the chief of the Seirim, or goat-demons, who haunted the desert and to whom most primitive Semitic (most likely non-Hebrew) tribes offered sacrifices. The Old Testament states that Jeroboam appointed priests for the Serim. But Josiah destroyed the places of their worship, as the practices accompanying this worship involved copulation of women with goats. The name Azazel may be derived from Azaz and El meaning "Strong one of God". It is thought that Azazel may have been derived from the Canaanite god, Asiz, who caused the sun to burn strongly. It has also been theorized that he has been influenced by the Egyptian god Set.

Azazel is Lucifer's most powerful son. Azazel is the Southern Crowned Prince of Hell. Azazel is a very important Demon as he is the son of Satan. He is the Chief Standard Bearer of the Infernal Army. Azazel works directly with Satan. He is in charge of top security in Hell. Azazel is the warrior God of justice, truth, and revenge. He is a Master of the Black Arts and a Protector of Travelers. Azazel is also my Unholy Guardian Demon.

Belial

Belial distributes presentations and titles. He reconciles friends and enemies and provides familiars. He can assist finding a job and helps to gain a higher position. He can bring favors from others, even one's enemies. Belial was Prince of the Order of Virtues. Belial is thin, smaller than most of the other Demons and has platinum blonde hair.

Belial is the Arch-Devil that rules over my birthday August 11.
Belial was the last demon to fall and the vilest葉he demon of impurity and lies. Belial is the King of Demons and Dark Spirits. This Demon King of the Nightside is a powerful Demon.

Leviatan

The name of this Dragon of the Void derives from Hebrew and means, "that which gather itself into folds" or "that which is drawn out." It is a sea monster that is the soul of the world, or Anima Mundi. Leviatan is the most dangerous monster that had to confront. Leviatan is a female Demon. She resembles a dragon with black eyes and sharp teeth, carrying the Antichrist on its back. The Antichrist draws his force from the beast he rides on, having seven heads and ten horns. Leviatan is both the Inner and Outer Dragon - the primal force of all creation and all destruction. Leviatan's other name is Tiamat, the Goddess worshiped

THROUGH USE OF THE SIMON NECRONOMICON.

Hecate

Hecate is the teacher of witchcraft and the guide to our personal underworld. She is the guardian of the mystical Crossroads. She shows us parts of ourselves that we are not aware of, that which has to be confronted and embraced in our personal initiatory process and she is an excellent guide for those practitioners who take their first steps on the path.

Asmodeus/Samael

Asmodeus or Samael is a Demonic King that is the Lord of Lust and Persian Demon of Wrath. He gives rings influenced by astronomical bodies, advises men on making themselves invisible and instructs men in the art of geometry, arithmetic, astronomy and the mechanical arts. He also knows of treasures.

He holds the title "King of the Demons".

Ninnghizhidda

Ninnghizhidda is the Necronomicon's Horned Serpent of the Deep and Watcher of the Gate of Cutha, the Land of the Lost. He is the Mesopotamian Deity of Vegetation and the Underworld. Ninnghizhidda is Sumerian for "Lord of the Good Tree" and is the offspring of Satan.

Sorath

Sorath is the son of Satan and the Demon of the Sun. He is said to have been Adolf Hitler's personal Guardian Demon and is very difficult to work with. He works with the section of the brain called the ID and you must be strong mentally in order to work with him. Sorath rules from the North and his colors are black and dark purple. Sorath holds the secret of all black magic and his number is 666.

Chapter 12: Pacts With the Devil

There are many ways to make a pact with Lucifer, but I'm going to go with the basics. There are four pacts you can do in order from the first to the fourth, but I only recommend the first one, because it's the best to go with. This is known as Dedicating Your Soul to Satan. If you want, you can make more than one pact.

How to Dedicate Your Soul to Satan

Get a clean piece of paper, large enough to write out the prayer below. If I were you, I would use parchment paper and Dragon's Blood ink. That would be best, because the paper is old-fashioned and the ink is legit and smells good to Demons.

Dragon's Blood ink is useful for writing down purpose, desires and intentions that will help to accelerate energies toward your goals. Dragon's Blood ink is just the right kind of ink to use when you're trying to make a pact with the Devil. Dragon's Blood ink is potent. Spells for any purpose are possible with this ink. It enhances all elements.

You have to perfect the pact and make it look really neat and your name has to be signed in blood perfectly. It has to be perfect so the Devil looks upon it favorably. You also have to renounce God, his son and rotten Holy Spirit in order to align yourself with the Forces of Darkness.

Write the following prayer below on a piece of parchment paper:

"Before the almighty and ineffable God Satan Lucifer and in the presence of all dread Demons of Hell, who are the True and the Original gods, I, (state your full name) renounce any and all past allegiances. I renounce the false Judeo/Christian god Jehova, I renounce his vile and worthless son Yeshua, I renounce his foul, odious and rotten Holy Spirit.

I proclaim Satan Lucifer as my one and only God. I promise to recognize and honor him in all things, without reservation, desiring in return, his manifold assistance in the successful completion of my endeavors and fulfillment of my desires."

Then after you get done writing it, take a long shower and make sure you get yourself completely clean and odor-free. Bathing before ritual is done out of respect. Dress in all black to show that you are serious about teaming up with the Forces of darkness. When you're ready, use a razor and cut the tip of your left pointer finger. Squeeze some blood out inside a little cap or something small. Dip the quirell pen or calligraphy pen in your blood and sign your name in blood. When you're done signing your name in blood, read the prayer out loud and then burn it in the flame of a blue, black or red candle. Meditate for about 15-30 minutes afterwards or until the candle burns out. When you get done meditating, say, "So mote it be," then a big, "HAIL SATAN!"

"Had I as many souls as there be stars, I'd give them all for Mephistopheles!"

-Dr. Faustus

Remember, dedicating your soul to Satan is a requirement, but the rest of these pacts with Lucifer are completely optional.

I recommend this second prayer to use as your second pact:

"I, (WRITE FULL NAME), do hereby dedicate myself unto (Demon's Name). By Satan - the infernal monarch and ruler of the elements - I do swear allegiance to (Demon's Name) forever hereafter. I will serve and work with you as you so ask. Accept me now as a dedicated servant to the elements of your design. I affix my seal below."

Create a sigil at the bottom of the piece of paper and sign your name in blood.

Burn the prayer and meditate for 10-15 minutes.

This is the third pact you can make with Lucifer:

"I, (FULL NAME), being of sound mind, do hereby ally and pact with Lucifer, the Devil Satan. I affirm that Satan is a powerful God with whom I am content to dedicating my soul to, as which seems appropriate. My loyalty is never-ending, my future is the fulfillment of my endeavors. Having on the date below signed this pact in my own blood, I affirm my part in our ongoing bond of mutual friendship. I let this pact symbolize the depth of my commitment to my alliance with Lucifer, Prince and Master of the Rebel Spirits. I sign this eternal oath in my own blood as a testament to my dedication."

Make an X then a line, signing your name in blood on the line

Burn it in the flame of a candle after reading out the prayer

This is the fourth pact you can make with Lucifer:

"In the name of the Dragon, I, (FULL NAME) acknowledge Lucifer to be my one and only true God. I promise to recognize Lucifer to be the Savior of Humanity and the Creator of All.
Lord of Thaumiel, embrace me in the realm of Sitra Ahra. Empower and protect my soul. Deliver me from all past error and delusion. Prince of Darkness, guide me on the Serpent Path to the heart of your Throne. Enter my body and liberate my soul. Reveal to me the secrets of the universe, secrets of Empyrean Heights and Infernal Depths. Wicked Serpent, seduce me with your promise of knowledge, so that I may walk the backwards path of the Devil into the Heart of Eternity."

Make an X followed by a line, signing your name in blood on the line

Read out loud the prayer then burn it in the flame of a blue, black or red candle

You can make more than one pact with a particular spirit and it always brings to closer to the spirit on a personal friendship level. I have made around 7 pacts with Satan Lucifer, each one swearing allegiance to the Devil, Master of the Rebel Spirits. Not only have I made pacts with Satan, but other powerful Demons such as Azazel and Asmodeus as well. The purpose of making multiple pacts with certain Demons is to attain personal power and knowledge and also form friendships with these Demons. The names of the Demons I've made pacts with are: Satan/Lucifer, Azazel, Baphomet, Nyarlathotep, Asmodeus/Samael, Lucifuge Rofocale, Belial, Leviatan/Tiamat, and others. I've attained a lot of true gnosis and power by signing such pacts with my name in blood. The Demons in which I favor most are Satan Lucifer, Azazel (my Guardian Demon), Asmodeus, Tiamat/leviatan and Nyarlathotep.

The best Spirit of Evil you definitely want to make a pact with first is, of course, Lucifer or Satan because he bestows magic powers and secret knowledge to those whom he favors. Satan or Lucifer is also known as Iblis, who in the religion of Islam, is the primary Spirit of Evil who is in charge of Djinn (Demons made of Smokeless Fire).

Chapter 13: The Devil's Keys

These are the 19 Enochian Keys of Lucifer. These Enochian Keys are revised from Joy of Satan, because Lucifer likes to be called by his name rather than his title "Satan". They are revised to be used by the Spiritual Luciferian. Beware of these Keys, for they are powerful!

First Key

I reign over you, saith Lucifer in power exalted above the firmaments and over the earth; in whose hands the sun is as a sword and the moon as a thorough-thrusting fire: Who measureth your garments in the midst of my vestures and trussed you together as the palms of my hands and brightened your vestments with infernal light. I made a law to govern my sons and daughters. I delivered truth and furnished to you the power of understanding. Moreover, ye lifted up your voices and swore obedience and faith to Satan Lucifer who liveth and triumpheth, whose beginning is not nor end cannot be. Who shineth as a flame in the midst of your palace and reigns amongst you as the balance of righteousness and truth. Move therefore and show yourselves! Open the mysteries of your creation! Be friendly unto me! For I am the

SERVANT OF THE SAME, THE TRUE WORSHIPER OF LUCIFER IN GLORY AND POWER EXALTED, OF THE KINGDOM OF THE SOUTH!

First Key (Enochian)

OL SONUF VORSAG GOHO LUCIFER LONSH CALZ OD VORS CAOSGO; SOBRA ZOL ROR I TA NAZPS OD GRAA TA MALPRG: DS HOL-Q QAA NOTHOA ZIMZ OD COMMAH TA NOBLOH ZIEN OD LUCIFTIAN OBOLEH DONASDOGAMATASTOS. O OHORELA TABA OL NORE OD PASBS OL ZONRENSG VAOAN OD TOOAT NONUCAFE GMICALZOMA. PILAH FARZM ZNRZA OD SURZAS ADNA OD GONO DE LUCIFER, DS HOM OD TOH. SOBA CROODZI IPAM UL VLS IPAMIS. DS LOHOLO VEP NOTHOA POAMAL OD BOGPA AAI TA PIAP PIAMOL OD VAOAN. ZACARE CA OD ZAMRAN! ODO CICLE QAA! ZORGE! ZIR NOCO! HOATH LUCIFER BVFD LONSH LONDOH BABAGE!

Second Key

CAN THE WINGS OF THE WINDS UNDERSTAND YOUR VOICES OF WONDER O YOU, SONS AND DAUGHTERS OF LUCIFER? OF WHOM HELL-FIRE HAS FRAMED WITHIN THE DEPTHS OF MY JAWS; WHOM I HAVE PREPARED AS A GATHERING FOR A WEDDING, OR AS THE FLOWERS IN THEIR BEAUTY FOR THE CHAMBERS OF PLEASURE. STRONGER

ARE YOUR FEET THAN THE BARREN STONE, AND MIGHTIER ARE YOUR VOICES THAN THE MANIFOLD WINDS; FOR YOU ARE BECOME A BUILDING SUCH AS IS NOT, SAVE IN THE MIND OF LUCIFER, THE ALL-POWERFUL. ARISE! MOVE THEREFORE UNTO HIS SERVANTS; SHOW YOURSELVES IN POWER, AND MAKE ME A STRONG SEER OF THINGS; FOR I AM OF LUCIFER WHO LIVES FOREVER!

SECOND KEY (ENOCHIAN)

ADGT VPAAH ZONG OM FAAIP SALD, NONCI NORE OD PASBS DE LUCIFER? SOBAM DONASDOGAMATASTOS IZAZAZ PIADPH; CASARMA ABRAMG TA ALDI PARACLEDA Q TA LORSLQ TURBS OOGE QVASAHI. GIVI CHIS LUSD ORRI, OD MICALP CHIS BIA OZONGON; LAP NOAN TROF CORS TA GE, O Q MANIN DE LUCIFER TOL-LONSH TORZU! ZACARE! CA C NOQOD; ZAMRAN MICALZO OD OZAZM VRELP LAP ZIR DE LUCIFER APILA GOHED!

Third Key

Behold! Saith Lucifer, I am a circle on whose hands stand twelve kingdoms. Nine are the seats of living breath the rest are as sharp sickles or the horns of death wherein the Creatures of Earth are and are not except by mine own hands, which also sleep and shall rise! In the beginning I made you stewards, and placed you in the twelve seats of government, giving unto every one of you power successively over the nine true ages of time, to the intent that, from the highest vessels and the corners of your governments, ye might work my power: pouring down the fires of life and increase continually upon the Earth. Thus ye are become the skirts of justice and truth. In Lucifer's name, rise up! Show yourselves! Behold! His mercies flourish! His name is become mighty among us! In whom we say move! Ascend! Apply yourselves unto us as unto the partakers of his mysteries in your creation!

Third Key (Enochian)

Micama goho Lucifer, zir comselh a zien biah os londoh. Em chis othil gigipah vnd-l chis ta pvim q mospleh teloch Qvi-in toltorg caosga chisi od chis ge m ozien, ds t brgdo od torzul! Acroodzi eol balzarg, od aala os thiln netaab, dlvga vomsarg Lonsa capmiali vors em homil cocasb, fafen izizop od miinoag de gnetaab, Vavn lonsh: Panpir malpirgi pild caosg noan vnalah balt od vooan. A Lucifer's dooain, torzu! Zamran! Micma! Iehvsoz ca-cacom! Dooain noar micaolz aai om! Casarmg gohia: zacar! Torzu! Imvamar pvgo! Pvgo plapli cicles qaan!

Fourth Key

I have set my feet in the South and have looked about me saying: Are not the thunders of increase numbered 666 which reign in the second angle? I have placed whom none hath yet numbered but two: in who the second beginning of things are and wax strong, which also successively, adding the numbers of time and their powers stand as in the beginning. Rise up ye sons of pleasure and visit the Earth, for I am of Lucifer who is and lives forever! In Lucifer's name, move! Show yourselves as pleasant deliverers that you may praise him

AMONGST THE SONS OF MEN!

FOURTH KEY (ENOCHIAN)

OTHIL LUSDI BABAGE OD DORPHA GOHOL: G-CHIS GE AVAVAGO CORMP MIAN, CORMP MIAN, OALI SOBAM AG CORMPO CRP VI-IV: CASARMG VIV CROODZI CHIS OD VGEG, DS T CAPIMALI COAZIOR GAPIMAON OD LONSHIN BIAH TA CROODZI EM! TORZU! NORE DE QVASAHI OD EF CAOSGA! LAP ZIR LUCIFER DS I OD APILA GOHED! I LUCIFER'S DOOAIP, ZACARE! ZAMRAN OBELISONG NONCI REST TOX AAF NORE MOLAP!

FIFTH KEY

THE MIGHTY SOUNDS HAVE ENTERED INTO THE FOURTH ANGLE AND ARE BECOME AS DELIVERERS OF LORD LUCIFER'S PROVIDENCE, BRINGING FORTH STRENGTH AND UNDERSTANDING DWELLING IN THE FIRMAMENTS AS CONTINUAL COMFORTERS; UNTO WHOM I FASTENED PILLARS OF GLADNESS 666, AND GAVE THEM VESSELS TO WATER THE EARTH WITH ALL HER CREATURES; AND THEY ARE THE SONS AND DAUGHTERS OF LUCIFER. OF THE FIRST AND THE SECOND AND THE BEGINNING OF THEIR OWN SEATS WHICH ARE GARNISHED WITH CONTINUAL BURNING LAMPS WHOSE NUMBERS ARE AS THE BEGINNING, THE

ends, and the contents of time. Therefore!
Come ye and appear to your creation! Visit
us in peace and comfort conclude us
receivers of your mysteries, for why? We
worship Lucifer in all his glory,
everlasting!

Fifth Key (Enochian)

Sapah zimii sdiv od noas obelisong de
Lucifer's yarry, iolcam vgear od
Gmicalzoma praf calz tablior; casarm
amipzi naz arth mian, Od dlvgar zizop zlida
caosgi toltorgi od z chis nor od Pasbs de
Lucifer. Talo od taviv od croodzi de thild ds
chis Gnonp peoal cormfa chis croodzi vls
od q cocasb ca! Niis od zacar Qaas!
Fetharsi od bliora ozazma ednas Cicles
bagle? Ge boalvah Lucifer bvsd, Gohed!

Sixth Key

The spirits of the fourth angle are nine, mighty in the Firmament of waters; whom the second hath planted as a torment to Jehova, and a garland to the sons and daughters of Lucifer, giving them fiery darts to winnow the earth and nine continual workmen whose courses visit with comfort, the earth, and are in government and continuance. Hearken to my voice! I have talked of you and I move you in power and presence whose works shall be a song of honor and the praise of Lucifer in your creation!

Sixth Key (Enochian)

Gah de sdiv chis em, micalzo pilzin de sobam; Casarm taviv harg ta mir iad, od obloc nore od pasbs de Lucifer, dlvgar malprg ar caosga od em canal sobol zar fbliard caosga, od chis netaab od miam. Solpeth bien! Brita od zacam gmicalzo sobha vavn trian lviahe od ecrin de Lucifer qaaon!

Seventh Key

The east is a house of harlots singing praises amongst the flames of first glory, wherein Lord Lucifer hath opened his mouth, and they are become 9 living dwellings in whom the strength of man rejoiceth; and they are appareled with ornaments of brightness, such as work wonders on all creatures; whose kingdoms and continuance are as the seven ziarahs, the mighty Towers of Lucifer, continual places of comfort; of joy everlasting. O ye servants of pleasure Move! Appear! Sing praises unto Lucifer! Be mighty amongst us; for to his remembrance is given power, and

OUR STRENGTH WAXETH STRONG IN THE COMFORT OF LUCIFER!

Seventh Key (Enochian)

Raas salman babalond oecrimi aao malprg croodzi bvsd, qviin Lucifer odo bvtmon od z chis noas em paradial casarmg vgear olora chirlan; od z chis zonac luciftian, cors ta vavl zirn tolhami; soba londoh od miam chis ta q ziarahs, micalz vmadea de Lucifer, pibliar; moz gohed. C no qvol de qvasahi, Zacare! Zamran! Oecrimi de Lucifer! Omicaolz aai om; bagle papnor dlvgam Lonshi, od vmplif vgegi blior de Lucifer!

Eighth Key

The mid-day, the fifth, is as in the Duat, made of pillars of hyacinth, in whom the Elders are become strong which I have prepared for my own justice saith Lucifer; who liveth and reigneth forever. Rejoice! In the glory of the Dragon that is triumphant and everlasting! How many are there which remain in the glory of the earth which are and shall not see death until Jehova doth fall and his followers doth sink? Come away! For the thunders have roared! Come away! For the temples and robe of Lucifer shall be crowned and are no longer divided. Come forth! Appear! unto the terror of the Earth, and to our comfort and of such as are prepared!

Eighth Key (Enochian)

Bazm, o, i ta a at, oln naz avabh, casarmg vran chis vgeg ds abramg baltim goho Lucifer; soba apila od bogpa gohed. Chirlan! A bvsd de vovim ar i homtoh od gohed! Irgil chis ds paaox i bvsd de caosgo ds chis od ip vran teloah cacrg iad gnai loncho od fafen gnai carbaf? Niiso! Bagle avavago yor! Niiso! Bagle siaion od mabsa de Lucifer trian momar od chis ripir poilp. Niis! Zamran! Ciaofi caosgo, od bliors od corsi ta chis abramig!

Ninth Key

A mighty guard of fire with two-edged swords flaming, which have vials of wrath and whose wings of wrath and whose wings are of wormwood and of the marrow of salt, have settled their feet in the south and are measured with their ministers 666. These gather up the moss of the earth as the rich man doth his treasure. Cursed are Jehova; he who sits on the holy throne and are his servants! Whose iniquities are in their eyes, millstones greater than the earth, and from their mouths rain seas of blood; their heads are covered with diamonds and upon their hands are marble sleeves. Happy is he on whom they frown not; for why? Lucifer rejoiceth in them. Come away! Leave your vials for the time is such as requireth comfort!

Ninth Key (Enochian)

Micaolz bransg prgel napta malpirgi, ds brin efafafe vonpho od sobca vpaah chis tatan od tranan balye, alar lusda babage od chis holq c noqvodi mian. Vnal aldon mom caosgo ta las ollor Gnai limlal. Amma chis Jehova; idoigo od chic noqodi! Sobca madrid chis ooanoan, aviny drilpi caosgin, od bvtmoni parm zvmvi cnila; daziz chis ethamz a childao od mirc ozol chis pidiai collal. Vlcinin a sobam vcim ip; Bagle? Lucifer chirlan par. Niiso! Bams ofafafe! Bagle a cocasb i cors ca vnig blior!

Tenth Key

The thunders of judgment and wrath are numbered and are harbored In the South. In the likeness of an oak whose branches are nests of lamentation and weeping laid up for Jehova and his servants, which burn night and day, and vomit out the heads of scorpions, and live sulphur mingled with poison. These are the thunders that roar with a hundred mighty earthquakes and a thousand times as many surges, which rest not, nor know any echoing time. Here one rock bringeth forth a thousand even as the heart of man does his thoughts. Woe!

Woe! Woe! Woe! Woe! Woe! Yeah Woe! Be to he who sits on the holy throne in heaven! His iniquity is, was and shall be great. Come away! But not your mighty sounds!

Tenth Key (Enochian)

Coraxo chis cormp od chis blans de babage. Aziazior paeb soba lilonon chis virq eophan od raclir maasi bagle iad od noqodi, ds ialpon dosig od basgim, od oxex daziz siatris, od salbrox cynxir faboan. Vnal chis const ds yor eors vohim gizyax od matb cocasg plosi molvi, ds page ip, larag om droln matorb cocasb. Emna l patralx yolci matb nomig monons olora gnay angelard. Ohio! Ohio! Ohio! Ohio! Ohio! Ohio! Noib ohio! Bolp idoigo madriax! Bagle iad madrid I, zirop od chiso drilpa. Niiso! Crip ip micalz apah!

Eleventh Key

The mighty seat groaned aloud and there were seven thunders and the eagle spake and cried with a loud voice: Come away from the house of death! And they gathered themselves together and be same those of whom it is measured; The everlasting ones, who ride the whirlwinds. Come away! For I have prepared a place for you. Move therefore and show yourselves! Open the mysteries of your Creation! Be friendly unto me for I am the servant of the same! The true worshiper of Lucifer in glory and power exalted Of the Kingdom of the South!

Eleventh Key (Enochian)

Oxiayal holdo od zirom q coraxo od vabzir camliax od bahal: Niiso salman teloch! Od par aldon od noan casarman holq; Gohed saga do zildar zong. Niiso! Bagle abramg pi noncp. Zacare ca od zamran! Odo cicle qaa! Zorge! Zir noco! Hoath Lucifer bvfd lonsh londoh babage!

Twelfth Key

O you that reign in heaven and are 3, the lanterns of sorrow bind up your girdles and shall be as bucklers to the stooping followers of Jehova! That Lord Lucifer may be magnified; whose name amongst you is wrath! Move therefore and show yourselves! Open the mysteries of your creation! Be friendly unto me! For I am the servant of the same! The true worshiper of Lucifer In glory and power exalted of the Kingdom of the South!

Twelfth Key (Enochian)

Nonci ds sonf madriax od chis d, hvbaio tibibp allar atraah od trian Ta lolcis abai Fafen de iad! Ar Lucifer ovof; soba dooain Aai i vonph! Zacare ca od zamran! Odo cicle qaa! Zorge! Zir noco! Hoath Lucifer bvfd lonsh londoh babage!

Thirteenth Key

O you swords of the South which have 42 eyes to stir up the pleasures of sin, making men drunken; Behold! The promise of Lucifer and His power, which is called amongst those in heaven, a bitter sting! Move therefore and show yourselves! Open the mysteries of your creation! Be friendly unto me! For I am the servant of the same! The true worshiper of Lucifer in glory and power exalted of the Kingdom of the South!

Thirteenth Key (Enochian)

Napeai babage ds brin vx ooaona lring qvasahi de doalim, eolis ollog orsba; micma! Isro de Lucifer! Od tox lonshi, ds i vmd aai priaz de madriax, grosb! Zacare ca od zamran! Odo cicle qaa! Zorge! Zir noco! Hoath Lucifer bvfd lonsh londoh babage!

Fourteenth Key

O you sons and daughters of Lucifer, who sit upon 24 seats vexing he who sits on the holy throne in heaven. Behold! The voice of Lucifer! The promise of Him who is called amongst you extreme justice! Move therefore and show yourselves! Open the mysteries of your creation! Be friendly unto me! For I am the servant of the same! The true worshiper of Lucifer in glory and power exalted of the Kingdom of the South!

Fourteenth Key (Enochian)

Nore od pasbs de Lucifer, ds trint mirc ol thil dods idoigo a madriax. Micma! Bial de Lucifer! Isro tox de i vmd aai baltim! Zacare ca od zamran! Odo cicle qaa! Zorge! Zir noco! Hoath Lucifer bvfd Lonsh Londoh Babage!

Fifteenth Key

O thou the governor of the first flame, beneath whose wings which weave the Earth with wrath: Which knowest and delivereth justice and truth. Prepare for the reign of Lucifer and His Kingdom on Earth! Move therefore and show yourselves! Open the mysteries of your creation! Be friendly unto me! For I am the servant of the same! The true worshiper of Lucifer in glory and power exalted of the Kingdom of the South!

Fifteenth Key (Enochian)

Ils tabaan l ialprt, orocha casarman vpaahi ds oado Caosgi vonph: ds omax od zonrensg baltim od vooan. Abramg sonf de Lucifer od londoh mirc caosg! Zacare ca od zamran! Odo cicle qaa! Zorge! Zir noco! Hoath Lucifer bvfd Lonsh Londoh Babage!

Sixteenth Key

O thou of the second flame the Houses of Hell which hast their beginning in glory, shalt comfort the just; who walkest on the earth with feet of fire; Mighty art Lucifer and his followers! Move therefore and show yourselves! Open the mysteries of your creation! Be friendly unto me! For I am the servant of the same! The true worshiper of Lucifer in glory and power exalted of the Kingdom of the South!

Sixteenth Key (Enochian)

Ils viv malpirgi salman de donasdogamatatastos ds acroodzi bvsd, bliorax balit; ds insi caosg lusdan pvrgel; Micalzo chis Lucifer od fafen! Zacare ca od zamran! Odo cicle qaa! Zorge! Zir noco! Hoath Lucifer bvfd Lonsh Londoh Babage!

Seventeenth Key

O thou third flame whose wings are thorns to stir up vexation in the kingdom of heaven. Who hast nine living lamps going before thee. Gird up thy loins and hearken! Move therefore and show yourselves! Open the mysteries of your Creation! Be friendly unto me! For I am the servant of the same! The true worshiper of Lucifer in glory and power exalted of the Kingdom of the South!

Seventeenth Key (Enochian)

Ils d ialprt soba vpaah chic nanba zixlay dodsih adohi de madriax. Ds brint em hvbaro tastax ilsi. Aldon dax od toatar! Zacare ca od zamran! Odo cicle qaa! Zorge! Zir noco! Hoath Lucifer bvfd Lonsh Londoh Babage!

Eighteenth Key

O thou mighty light and burning flame of comfort which unveileth the glory of Lucifer unto the center of the earth, in whom the great secrets of truth have their abiding that is called in thy kingdom. Strength through joy and is not to be measured. Be thou a window of comfort unto me. Move therefore and appear! Open the mysteries of your creation! Be friendly unto me for I am the servant of the same! The true worshiper of Lucifer in glory and power exalted of the Kingdom of the South!

Eighteenth Key (Enochian)

Ils micaolz olpirt od malprg bliore ds odo bvsd de Lucifer ovoars caosgo, casarmg micaolz cicles vooan brints Cafafam ds i vmd a q londoh vgear de moz od maoffas. Bolp como bliort pambt. Zacare ca od zamran! Odo cicle qaa! Zorge! Zir noco! Hoath Lucifer bvfd Lonsh Londoh Babage!

Nineteenth Key

O you Demons who dwell upon and are mighty governors of the Earth, who execute the judgment of Lucifer! To you it is said: Behold the face of Lucifer, The beginning of comfort, whose eyes are the brightness of the stars; who provided you for the government of the Earth, and her variety, furnishing you with a power of understanding, to dispose all things according to the providence of he who reigneth on the Throne from Hell and rose up in the beginning, saying: The Earth, let her be governed by her parts. The course of her, let it run with pleasure, and as a handmaid let her serve Lucifer. One season, let it confound another; and let there be no creature upon or within her the same. All her members, let them differ in their qualities; And let there be no one creature equal with another. The reasonable creatures of the Earth, let them vex and weed out one another; and the dwelling places. The works of the followers of Jehova and his pomp, let them be defaced. The buildings of he who sits on the holy throne, let them become caves for the beasts of the field; their iniquities shall be known. For why? I regret their creation. O you sons and daughters of Lucifer, arise! Those in the kingdom of heaven, let them serve you. Govern those that govern; cast down such as fall; bring

FORTH JUSTICE AND DESTROY THE ROTTEN. NO PLACE LET IT REMAIN IN ONE NUMBER; ADD AND DIMINISH, UNTIL THE STARS BE NUMBERED. ARISE, MOVE! APPEAR BEFORE LUCIFER! HE HAS SWORN UNTO US HIS JUSTICE; OPEN THE MYSTERIES OF YOUR CREATION, AND MAKE US PARTAKERS OF UNDEFILED TRUTH.

NINETEENTH KEY (ENOCHIAN)

ILS DAEMONS DS PRAF OD CHIS MICAOLZ ARTABAS DE CAOSGO, DS FIFIS BALZIZRAS DE LUCIFER! NONCA GOHVLIM: MICAM ADOIAN DE LUCIFER, ACROODZI BLIORB, SOBA OOAONA CHIS LUCIFTIAS AOIVEAE; DAS ABRAASA NONCF NETAAIB CAOSGI, OD TILB DAMPLOZ, TOOAT NONCF G MICALZ OMA, LRASD TOLGLO MARB YARRY DE TOX BOGPA OXIAYAL LONDOH BABAGE OD TORZULP ACROODZI, GOHOL: CAOSGA, TABAORD SAANIR. ELZAP TILB, PARM GI QVASAHI, OD TA QVRLST BOOAPIS LUCIFER. L NIMB, OVCHO SYMP; OD CHRISTEOS AG TOLTORN MIRC Q TIOBL LEL. TON PAOMBD, DILZMO ASPIAN; OD CHRISTEOS AG L TOLTORN PARACH A SYMP. CORDZIZ DODPAL OD FIFALZ L SMNAD; OD FARGT, A VA DE FAFEN DE JEHOVA OD AVAVOX, TONVG. ORSCA DE IDIGO, NOASMI TABGES LEVITHMONG; MADRID TRIAN OMAN. BAGLE? MOOOAH QAAN. NORE OD PASBS DE LUCIFER, TORZU! PRIAZ ADOHI DE MADRIAX, ABOAPRI. TABAORI PRIAZ AR TABAS; ADRPAN CORS TA DOBIX; YOLCAM BALIT OD QVASB QTING. RIPIR PAAOXT SAGA COR; VML OD PRDZAR, CACRG AOIVEAE CORMPT. TORZU,

ZACAR! ZAMRAN ASPT LUCIFER! SURZAS TIA BALTAN; ODO CICLE QAA, OD OZAZMA PLAPLI VOOAN.

VULGATA FINIS LUCIFERI

END OF THE GRIMOIRE
THE LUCIFERIC BIBLE

www.ingramcontent.com/pod-product-compliance
Ingram Content Group UK Ltd.
Pitfield, Milton Keynes, MK11 3LW, UK
UKHW010716300725
7143UKWH00026B/93